Stepping Beyond Judgment

Lynn M. Bunch

Phoenix, Arizona

First Printing, April 2001
Second Printing, January 2005
Third Printing, March 2010
Fourth Printing, January 2018

ISBN-13: 978-1983658334
ISBN-10: 1983658332

Published by Intuitive Ink
320 E. Virginia Avenue, Suite 202 Phoenix AZ 85004
Tel: (602) 621-4027
Fax: (602) 621-4032
Email: info@intuitivedevelopment.org
Website: http://www.intuitivedevelopment.org

To order any of Lynn's books visit our website for more information.

Other Works By Lynn M. Bunch:

Books
Divine Wisdom

Course Curriculum
Understanding Emotional Patterns
Defining Bottom Lines
7 Human Roles
Embracing Your Truth
Discovering Your Life Purpose
Releasing Old Beliefs
Merging Lives
Manifesting Your Desires
Spirit World
Blueprint Integration

Dedication

This book is dedicated to Archangel Michael. Thank you for your patience while awaiting my return.

Acknowledgements

My heartfelt gratitude goes to:

My sons Jacob and Adam, for their commitment to me and for sacrificing many hours of family time. I am honored to be your mother.

My mom and dad for their commitment and love to each other, our family, and the world.

My sister, Lisa, and our spiritual kinship. Thanks for keeping our dream alive.

My nephew and niece Boston and Marley, for sharing their mother.

My grandchildren for allowing me to become the best Nana I can be.

My friends who have endured many changes throughout the years and loved me through and through.

My clients, without whom I would still be working at my day job—only dreaming of making a living doing what I love.

Contents

Preface

The intuitive work I have been doing on my life's journey is true to my heart. If there is anything that I share in my writings that feels right to you, please put it to use in your own life path, and, if for some reason it does not, leave it be. We are all very different and our differences must be celebrated. Our experiences are our own, never to be judged as wrong by ourselves or anyone else.

My desire in writing this book began with an empty heart that needed to be remembered. I have lived a great deal of my life for everyone else's approval, love, and acceptance. I have found in my quest for self-love that I am not alone. If on any level, my story can reach someone else's heart and help them to remember themselves in a way that they have forgotten, my mission will be fulfilled.

I began this book by simply writing. I did not know at the time that it would be a book; it was simply my way of expressing the teachings and dialogue I was having with my Guardian Angel. At some point in my writing, however, I was told I would be sharing this with many others. Of course, that scared me, as I am sure it would scare anyone. The exposure itself was enough to stop me right in my tracks.

When I was told I would be sharing myself on such a large scale, the fear was immobilizing. I can honestly say I was following through with this divine plan, but not without protest. My mind could not let go of the fact that I was going to have to deal with a large arena of people who would be questioning my intent, integrity, and, frankly, my sanity. This was not easy when I first began my business, and I was not looking forward to the scrutiny.

Exposure has always been my biggest fear. When I began my new career, I hurtled through a great deal of self-doubt and fear about appearing "different" in my private sessions, and my experience was often that as soon as clients were sitting with me in a session they had the benefit of seeing the whole picture; I actually was this confident, loving, and very normal wife and mother who had simply embraced her gifts. But now, putting my life experiences in writing would be something altogether different. My reluctance, to say the least was HUGE! I can only say that the nudge, or should I say PUSH, to overcome that reluctance was ultimately bigger. Many of my writings are teachings that what I will refer to as "spirit guides" have expressed through me and the rest are the experiences I have received in being connected to them.

I could not have written this book without the incredible help I have received from everyone that has interacted with me in assisting my forward progress. There have been numerous people in my life that have been instrumental in my growth, many who have no idea of their impact on my life, but also many who do understand, and I am forever thankful for all of their participation in my journey.

I am in no way finished with my journey of self-love. I hope to continue to find many different ways in which I will expand, express, and experience my human existence. For all who read my writings, I ask only that you begin with an open heart. My wish is that I touch your heart and help you on your movement to higher consciousness.

Prologue

This book's intent is to allow all of us the ability to embrace a world of peace, harmony, and love, beyond anything we can imagine. All humans have had a time when they experienced their hearts. The heart is where our connection to the non-physical realm is located. "God," Universal Energy, the angelic and spirit realm, (it does not and never will matter to me what word you use to reconcile this concept); whatever Higher Source you may define for yourself, they are all located in the heart. This has been forgotten for a great many years, so we have become accustomed to believing that our minds are in control. This concept is not wrong, yet in the end, it leaves us unfulfilled. The logic of the mind, or "logical mind," is a very important aspect of who we are, though the Universe never intended it to be in control. My understanding is that if we transform our flow of Mind, Body, and Spirit, to Spirit, Mind, and Body, we will experience life's existence at greater and more effective levels.

Many people have experienced communication from the non-physical realm and made the transition to Spirit, Mind, and Body, and many are still transitioning. This transition alone will bring about the shift in consciousness that is necessary for our planet to survive in a peaceful, loving existence. The truth is that communication with the non-physical realm will be the norm. Judgment is the killer of Higher Consciousness.

We fall into misalignment with "God," or "Higher Source," when we judge ourselves or others. I could stop writing now, if only all humans could integrate this one concept. I do not mean that "God" is not present within us; I mean that we literally move out of the alignment, or connection, with "Higher Source" when we judge My intention in putting my teachings into print are to allow others the vision I have been given, along with the necessary tools, to move smoothly from pain, struggle, and fear into divine wisdom.

I am in no way defining these teachings. They are not of any religious or specific belief system; they are simply tools for reaching beyond the judgments of your logical mind into the love inside your heart and soul. The potential for the world to come is amazing, and the following pages are permeated with the blessing that you too can enjoy the peace and love that is available in Stepping Beyond Judgment, back into your heart.

1

My Roots

My parents moved to Phoenix, Arizona from Akron, Ohio in November of 1962 with their 3-month-old daughter, Lisa, my older sister, in tow. My parents met in kindergarten class, started dating in high school, and had a brief separation when Mom moved to Arizona after graduating high school. I believe it was during their exchange of letters that Dad realized he longed for life in the West.

With minimal money, they courageously packed their life, including Lisa, and followed their hearts to Phoenix, Arizona—the land of cowboys and Indians. Both of their extended families balked at the idea, questioning their sanity. At that time, people in the Midwest and back East had little knowledge of what the desert actually looked like and either pictured gunfights at the OK Corral or vast areas of nothing but sand. Undaunted, they made their dream a reality.

My story begins two and a half years later, on January 26, 1965. The son my father wanted, or so I grew up believing, was not to be. My mother and father are both very devoted, loving parents. However, as with a lot of men, my father longed for a son to carry on the family name and do the things guys do with sons. Everyone was sure I was a boy; so sure, in fact, that everything Mom received at my baby shower was done up in blue: blue blankets, blue clothes, blue books—you get the drift. Imagine their surprise when out popped pink, little me!

My father is one of those guys who lives and breathes cars. He's made his living in the automotive industry his entire life, and although he also owns and rides motorcycles, cars are his passion. On the day of my birth, Dad was in the waiting room when the doctor came out to give him the news of my arrival. As only car buffs can do, they ended up discussing the doctor's car, until finally, Dad realized he didn't yet know about my arrival. The doctor informed him that he was indeed the proud father of a six-pound baby girl. My father responded, "Great Doc, now about those tires." It's a story that has been told frequently throughout my life, for its supposed humor, yet, each time I heard it, the message I received was, "You were not wanted. I wanted a boy, not another girl."

My perception? My father wanted a son, but instead, got me. My judgment? He would have loved me more if I were a boy. Years later, after many teachings and lessons, I have pieced together how the perceptions and judgments of our stories, and the people in them, disrupt our connection with "God."

The emotions that my feelings of being unwanted provoked were devastating. I felt alone and unworthy.

Fortunately, through the love of my father and the love of myself, I now know that was never the truth. Indeed, it was only what I perceived to be the truth. Distinguishing perception from truth doesn't necessarily ease the pain of our experiences, but once understood, healing can begin.

I grew up in a middle-class family home with three bedrooms and one bathroom. Boy, was that one bathroom difficult for my father! Living with three girls, getting his turn in the bathroom wasn't easy. Our house was very average. It was blue with white trim on the outside with two big evergreen trees in the front, a single Ocotillo cactus between them, and to the right of the yard, three Aloe Vera plants. All the neighborhood kids hung out in front of our house. We played many games in the front yard at dusk, just as the sun was going down and the desert heat was subsiding. Typical games like *Red Rover, Red Light-Green Light,* and *Statues* were our favorites.

Our house continued to be the favorite hangout throughout high school. In fact, it wasn't only kids who gravitated to us. I can remember my family waking up one morning to find several of my dad's buddies from Akron in their sleeping bags on our front lawn. They had made an impromptu trip to Arizona, arrived in the wee hours of the morning, and camped out until we awoke to discover them. Our neighbors were either used to such odd comings and goings, or we were very well liked. Probably both. It wasn't our house that attracted people; it was our family. We've always been a very loving, hospitable, and heartfelt family; all who entered our home felt the love present there.

One very unique thing about our house was the kitchen. My mom got an itch for something new, so to express herself, she picked her kitchen colors of Chinese red and hot pink. The brick wall was painted hot pink, with a spattering of the bricks featuring Chinese red, along with the side door and cabinets. You could see these colors beaming through the kitchen window if you were driving down the street at night. My mother joked that it was like a beacon, calling to all who passed. She loved her kitchen, the beacon, and all its brightness. Yet, I think the incessant teasing from others started to weigh on her. Later in life, she was forever asking my dad to repaint it.

My dad was, and still is to this day, an insomniac. Since Dad was always up throughout the night, he would paint or do some other creative endeavor that my mom had expressed a desire for, so we'd often awaken to new and exciting surroundings. We didn't have a lot of extras after the necessities, but re-painting always kept our house cheerful and bright. Life in my house was never dull.

My parents have been married for more than half a century. To say I admire their marriage would not be completely honest: what I do admire about my parents' marriage is the true love that lies at the core of their commitment to each other. They are an example of two people on a quest for remembering their spirit within the commitment of marriage. This has caused great pain and great amounts of growth for our family, and I have learned much from both of them. They have been an explosive combination at times. When they experienced hard times, the whole family experienced hard times. Mom could be both the detonator and peacemaker, and Dad the TNT and fire extinguisher.

I can't relate how many times my sister and I would be hauled out of bed, at all hours of the night and pre-dawn mornings, to have a "family meeting." We would cringe whenever the light switch would be turned on, knowing we were going to be tired at school, come morning. These meetings could last for hours, and many times by their end, we couldn't even recall the purpose for the meeting in the first place. I suppose when you're not able to sleep and are wide-awake with something burning on your mind, it's hard to understand that others are not experiencing the same phenomena.

Dad's insomnia was both a curse and a blessing. The blessing was the impossibility of ever sneaking in after curfew, thereby keeping us out of unnecessary trouble. Of course, we didn't quite see it that way back then. However, the good times were as wondrous as the hard times were intense. The support they have given me throughout my life is, without a doubt, the most committed love that I could ever ask for.

When we come into this world, we believe that our parents are gods in female and male forms. As life continues, we slowly awaken to the realization that Mom and Dad are merely human beings. For some, this awakening occurs at a very young age. For others, this truth eludes them throughout their life. At some point, all that we have learned from these wonderful, honorable people is how to cope or not to cope in life. We see their different attributes and get to choose what we wish to further and what we wish to leave behind.

My father is compassionate, kind and loving. When there's an emergency, he stays calm and level- headed: he is a man you want around in a crisis. He has been a leader both in our family and in the community. He always made sure that we never wanted for anything and instilled a sense of responsibility and respect for our family name and ourselves. My dad still to this day makes a difference in all he undertakes.

Dad has always been patriotic and wanted to be of service to his country. Since he had no war to serve in, he decided to serve his community. When I was about five years old, my father joined the Phoenix Reserve Police Department. He did undercover work at night in "The Deuce," downtown Phoenix, which at that time was not a pretty place to be after dark. After winning the "Police Officer of the Year" award twice in a row, he was asked to leave the reserves and join the police force full-time. However, my dad refused, saying that he chose to contribute his time, without pay, to the reserves to do his part in serving his country. I am proud to say that my dad served for eight years with an exemplary record.

It was toward the end of his eight-year tenure that he started getting burnt out on the system and its inefficiencies. He would put criminals in jail, only to find them back on the streets, sometimes within a matter of hours, laughing in his face. Feeling himself becoming hard and cold towards all people, not just criminals, and seeing how his attitude affected our family, he stepped down. Of course that didn't stop my dad from participating elsewhere.

Dad next participated with our schools, getting to know the teachers and principals by name, working on different committees, and even christening our neighborhood park. He was also a member of the Lions Club and held a seat on the board of the Better Business Bureau. At one time, he owned a Texaco gas station, and then he was a service advisor at a major Chevrolet dealership. He then started a company that developed courses for teaching women a basic understanding of vehicle maintenance in order to protect them from being ripped off. The course was called "Under the Hood with Doug Lahood" and it was adopted statewide by different Chevrolet dealerships.

Dad next started a family-owned limousine company, La Limousine, where the whole family worked at one time or another. In my twenties, I became its general manager for the last five years of the thirteen years we were in business.

Dad has always been a "hands-on" kind of guy who loves to work with his hands, literally. He welded metal sculptures, and we went around the state to different art shows, seeing and meeting different people from all over the country. At home he painted a lot of portraits of our family and friends, and encouraged us to try our hand at it too, though my sister and I preferred the "paint by number" kits. This is the dad I experienced throughout child- hood and into adulthood, and as wonderful as he is, there is also the side of him that is explosive and combative. As a child, I rarely had direct experience with his temper, but I did experience the volatile fall-out between my sister and him. Then again, what else could you expect from a daughter who was a smaller, female version of him (more about this later).

Then there was my mother. I had a quiet camaraderie with my mother that no one really understood, which, quite frankly, angered my sister to no end. I spent a lot of time on my mother's lap when I was little, giving and receiving energy at the same time. Often, in lieu of words, we communicated through our spirits. I knew that deep down she understood what my tea parties meant to me (the topic of Chapter Two), so she encouraged them as much as she knew how to.

Mom was the quiet force of our family without which we couldn't have survived or thrived, perennially keeping the peace and us together.

It didn't exactly look like this from the outside, because Mom didn't say a lot, even when backed into a corner, but when she did speak, we listened. She knew when to speak and when not to; she understood how silence often conveys more than words. She is an amazing woman who all of my friends wanted as their mom and to this day see her as their second mom.

My dad was the parent who usually came to different events at school because of his flexible schedule; but, if I ever needed Mom, all I had to do was say so, and she would be there. I can't relate many vivid recollections of anything in particular that my mom did or said to convey her role as a peacemaker; it was simply the balance and peace within her that spoke volumes. Suffice it to say that my parents skillfully blended their parenting skills, and I can't imagine my life without either of them.

In addition to my parents and me, my sister was also an important factor in my childhood. She and I shared a bedroom, off and on, depending on who was visiting or living with us at the time. We spent the majority of our childhood in the same room until I was in seventh grade and we moved to bigger house.

Lisa always knew her position as the older sibling, and therefore felt as though I was born to serve her. She was the messiest person in the world, and I was the cleanest—at least in my opinion. We were like Felix and Oscar, The Odd Couple, all over again. In fact, that's what we were called.

My mom started working when I was in the second grade, which left Lisa and I with a baby-sitter after school. Things were fairly equal with a baby-sitter to keep the peace. But, after we turned old enough to be left at home alone, I became the servant, with Lisa as my lord and master. If she wanted to watch something on television, but I wanted something else, there was no democracy. She was far more stubborn than I was, and despite "rules of the house," most were not followed by Lisa.

We were not allowed to have people in the house while our parents were at work. However, being two-and-a-half years older, Lisa reached the "boy crazy" stage way before me, so she and her friends would have their boyfriends over to hang on the back porch, listening to music and smoking cigarettes. I thus began to use my newfound power of "If you don't let me___, I'm telling Mom and Dad...," and the scale became far more balanced in my favor; I had figured out the power of blackmail. But until that point, she was definitely in charge.

My sister, I am convinced, is a gift from "God." I can honestly say she is my very best friend in the world. Undeniably, this was not always the case. Our true friendship began after the birth of my first son, Jacob. Prior to that, we were sisters and nothing more. We shared the same parents, house, family, pets, etc, but there was nothing remotely close between us. If she liked chocolate, I liked vanilla, and it didn't stop there.

Watching Lisa was like watching a movie and seeing cause and effect, directly and clearly. I remember watching her interactions with our parents and consciously saying to myself, "Thank you for showing me what not to do and possibly saving my life in the process."

Because of her experiences, Lisa helped me see aspects of my personality that I decided not to delve into deeply. In our early years of growing up, she chose to learn the "hard way" or from so-called "negative" experiences. Thankfully, this is no longer true. The book, Course in Miracles, refers to our greatest teachers as "petty tyrants." Lisa was mine in my early childhood, and she has been this for so many other people in her life.

Lisa is extremely strong willed and will not allow anyone to take that away from her. What an inspiration!

This contrarian nature, however, can and has been at times destructive to herself and anyone opposing her. She was forever saying to me, "'Miss Perfect doesn't do anything wrong." I reasoned, Why would I, when the consequences always played out before my eyes? I learned quickly to "not even go there." She didn't realize what a gift she was to me, and at that time, neither did I. She was, and still remains, a wonderful teacher for me.

When I said Lisa has a side into which I choose not to delve, I was referring to the "dark" side that exists in each of us. However, unlike many, at that time, she was afraid to embrace the "light" side of herself. Even in our childhood, I can see how we balanced one another, unconsciously. She and my father would enter a test of wills, trying to hold tightly to their own position, while breaking down the other. Lisa and Dad have always had a way of provoking one another by their mere presence and often, neither will back down from confrontation.

I remember an instance when I was about 15 years old and Lisa was 17. We were standing in front of our laundry room door. She and my father were raging at one another. They are both very physical individuals and both were completely out of control a nasty combination. I was begging her to apologize, to make it better. However, I knew that wasn't going to happen. My dad took her head and pushed it into the door, punching a hole in it. Luckily for Lisa, the door was hollow, not solid oak. Lisa refused to cry. She always refused to cry. I cried for her.

Lisa went through her childhood refusing to let my dad see her pain while I went through mine absorbing it for her. I shared my light with her in the only way she would allow me, by feeling it for her. On the other hand, she embodied the injustice and rage that I kept bottled up inside the part of me that was too afraid to speak out, for fear of the consequences and also with the fear of being noticed. We have since worked diligently over the years at consciously embracing both sides of ourselves, forgiving the darkness, and empowering the light we possess.

2

The Tea Party

One of my most cherished childhood memories is of my tea parties. When I was about two or three years old, my Grandma Nema brought me a china tea set on one of her visits from Ohio. It was beautiful, dainty, and elegant, featuring white porcelain with yellow and gold flowers imprinted on the cups and saucers. Its beauty spoke to my heart. I would set up four impeccable place settings in my room on a small table for me and three of my friends. My friends and I would sit at that table for hours, chatting and solving the world's problems. There were times when I would include our dog, Caesar, in our parties, but, usually, it was just the four of us. People would come into my room and ask, "Lynny, who are you talking to?"

Eventually, I realized I was the only one that experienced my friends — the only one who saw them sitting right there at my table. Many people called them imaginary, but I knew there was nothing imaginary about them. They were as real to me as the family with whom I lived. I *knew* they existed.

I would get lost in my tea-party world for hours at a time until my sister or Mom would come into my room and interrupt me. I would then abruptly stop talking to my friends. At the time, I had no clue that my guests were the Archangels Michael, Gabriel and Raphael. My mother would chuckle at how cute I looked and my sister would make fun of me in that condescending way that only she can do. I was astounded at being regarded as "cute." After all, I was having a very serious conversation with friends. My tea parties received a lot of attention from others. They would say, "Oh, look how cute she is, sitting there with her make-believe friends. Look how intense she is."

I would think, *What are they talking about? I'm not talking to myself. Can't you see the other people here?* I saw nothing cute, unusual, or "make believe" about my tea parties. They were as important to me as eating or breathing, an integral part of who I was in life, fulfilling me more than anything else. I enjoyed playing games with other children, but my tea parties nurtured my soul.

At first I didn't pay much attention to those on the outside looking in. In fact, I probably wasn't even aware that anyone else was present, other than my friends. Eventually, however, the constant teasing permeated my inner world, and I became self-conscious about myself, my friends, and the attention we attracted. I say "attracted" because everyone was drawn to watching me, especially my mother and sister, and also to mimicking my mannerisms and words. Imitating me, they would crook their arm in my fashion and say, "Would you like some tea?"

Of course, I now know why. They wanted to be a part of the light that was radiating within us. They thought I was playing "pretend"; whereas, I thought they were making fun of me. Although I have a very loving family, their mockery of me was undoubtedly arising from ignorance; they were not deliberate attempts to hurt me. Nevertheless, at the age of five, I made a decision to never be made fun of again. My tea parties became a thing of the past. My heart closed up shop.

Little did I know, in making that decision, that I had willed the angels and spirits to leave me alone, thereby closing off my connection to that realm for many, many years. In the ensuing years, I felt isolated and alone, even when surrounded by people. My inner world became barren until, in complete desperation, while standing in the shower one day, I called upon "God" to reveal Archangel Michael to me. And fortunately, I was heard: one of my dear, dear friends did return.

3

Waking Up

My journey back to my heart started at the age of 25. I had been working at being a better person by going to counseling, reading self-help books, listening to tapes, and so on. However, the true quest for self-love and a connection to a higher source did not pull at my heart until my second child Adam was born. After his birth, I was in a semi-numb state of satisfaction. I believed I had all a person could want: two beautiful children, a husband I loved, a nice home, dependable cars, and a well-paying job.

My accomplishments seemed great when compared to a lot of people, yet, something was missing: the fulfillment that these experiences were supposed to bring. My experiences weren't mirages, they could have been completely fulfilling, but they weren't. I felt a void within. I found myself living the life I had always thought would bring me happiness, not knowing what I would eventually learn is the true source of happiness.

I began my journey to fulfilling happiness with small steps such as going to church, reading any self-help books

I could get my hands on, and forcing myself to become consciously aware of what was really going on in my life. It was no longer okay to ignore the hurtful words my husband was hurling at me, the fact that he wasn't coming home until late at night, or the reality that his drug use was running rampantly out of control. However, I dutifully continued trying to ignore these facts for a few more years, desperately hoping that I would be able to grow spiritually within my failing marriage. But this was not sustainable nor possible. Finally, after seven years of marriage, it was time to wake up.

One day I had to return home early because I had forgotten my checkbook. It's funny how "God" intervenes. I came home early to find my husband, Kirk, and his friend doing lines of cocaine on our glass dining room table. Completely shocked and feeling betrayed at his total disregard for our family, I began screaming at him, "What if I had sent one of the boys after my checkbook? Get your things and get out!"

Kirk did leave. I'm sure his shame and relief of not having to hide his indiscretions had motivated him as much as my insistent declarations to do so. This was the first step of a very messy battle that became gut wrenching, painful, and ultimately, a blessing for everyone in our lives.

Despite his behavior, I loved Kirk with all my heart; we had been high school sweethearts. However, I use that term loosely, because if you had seen the fights we had been having for three-and-a-half years prior to our marriage, "sweet-hearts" would not have been an accurate description.

Should I have known better before marrying him? Yes. But, when you do not respect yourself, you do not expect anyone else to either. Neither one of us respected one another nor ourselves.

None of this is all that surprising, in retrospect. After all, we had both experimented with drugs in and shortly after high school. When we married, I was 20 and Kirk was 22. I had merely assumed that our experimental drug use was a phase, and adulthood lay ahead. I didn't want to continue with any experimentation, but I took for granted that Kirk felt the same. Unfortunately, what I considered "dabbling," he considered a way of life. It was such an obvious, deep wedge between us that no counselor could help. We tried many counselors, five to be exact. We were stubborn, but not naïve: the love of our hearts was present, we were simply not making the same choices, so the odds of continuing to try seemed futile.

I am sure had I asked, prior to marriage, if he ever planned to quit smoking pot and using other, harder drugs, Kirk would have told me "no." It's ironic that often in life, we never ask the questions to which we already know the answers. Now I see it all so clearly: I wasn't willing to ask, because I desperately loved him and knew that I would have to move on if I ever did find out the truth. The day I found him at the dining room table was the answer I had been ignoring, loud and clear. From that day forward, I grew: I began to love my boys and myself even more.

No matter how much it hurt, I knew I had to move on. Kirk left, as I had requested, and we proceeded to go through many battles until our divorce was finally granted almost two years later. During those two years, like many others do in times of seemingly unwanted change, I tried to reconcile my marriage for the sake of my boys as well as the dream I kept deep in my heart. However, finding pictures of my soon-to-be ex-husband with another woman, nearly being strangled to death by him, having him point a loaded gun at me, and a wake-up call visit by the police summarily ended any and all illusions of ever establishing the family my heart so desired. The battle scars became distinctly visible.

Thankfully, our boys have remained balanced through the years due to the love and support they have received from the love of family and "God." Adam and Jacob are fabulous young men, each capable of taking on the many unique hurdles that life has and will throw at them too.

4

In Search of the Light

I dated a bit after my divorce and contemplated marriage again, with Troy, a man who had been a long- time friend of my sister's husband (at the time). Muddling the situation, however, was the fact that through our family connection, Troy had also gained a friendship of sorts with Kirk. I loved Troy and he loved me, but Troy had a difficult time dealing with Kirk's overt hostility. This ultimately put too much of a strain on our relationship for it to survive.

Eventually, after waiting all day and night for a call from Troy on Valentine's Day, and receiving none, I felt enormously let down. I will never forget that night. I finally called him, in a last ditch effort to salvage what I already knew was unsalvageable. I called because I still had naïve hope for his warmth and a sincere excuse for his having forgotten the day that is a celebration of the heart. The phone call netted none of the above.

I felt discouraged: I had done so much work on myself, I had actually made a list of what I needed in a relationship. I had listed the qualities and criteria that I was willing to compromise on, and those that were non-negotiable, bottom lines. I was sure that since I had candidly offered my list to "God," he had sent me this special relationship with Troy, a relationship that met all of my heart's desires.

Unfortunately, whereas I was willing to follow through with what was needed to fulfill my heart, Troy, at that time, was unwilling to fulfill what his heart wanted. The result was an aching heart, but I made my peace with reality: I knew that it was time to move on and add another bottom line to my wish list: a willing participant. "God" happily answered my prayers about three hours later with a phone call from a man who would soon become my second husband.

When I heard the phone ring, I let the answering machine pick it up, thinking it was Troy. Our relationship was over, and I knew there was nothing more to say. When I heard the caller's voice, I flew across my bed and grabbed the phone. I was shocked at my own reaction. *What was I doing?* I knew the caller as an acquaintance; why was I diving for the phone? He wasn't even my type, or so I thought. When I asked him why he called now, at this exact time, on this exact date, he said the magic words that touched my heart, "I knew it was time."

I had first met Jeff about a year prior to his call, and had I developed the confidence in my spiritual connections that I now possess, I would not have been so surprised by my reaction to hearing his voice on the answering machine that day. There was an important connection between us, and in hindsight, I know that Michael had directed our introduction because in that brief moment, a year before this phone call, I had had a premonition that Jeff would be the man I was going to marry.

Many would think I should have embraced this kind and obvious message, however, Jeff's physical resemblance to my first husband, Kirk, was enough to make my logical mind run in the opposite direction as fast as it could possibly move.

My mind was effective in its spiritual denial: during that first year of our acquaintanceship, I would run into him from time to time, at friends' houses and various gatherings, somehow never giving the premonition and our connection much thought. I was therefore totally surprised by not only the timing of the phone call, but my visceral reaction regarding the need to answer the phone.

We talked and talked throughout the night, enchantedly remaining on the phone until the wee hours of the morning, sharing ourselves in a way that was beyond anything I had experienced with any man up until that point. Jeff was able to understand the deep intuitive part of me, a part that I had tried to hide from the world since the day I stopped my tea parties, the part of me that simply "knows" what people are feeling, and in return, I was fascinated with his ability to see colors around people when looking at them (at the time, he did not know that these are called auras). His belief system and honesty about his metaphysical experiences gave me the courage to look deeper into myself and ultimately find my truth once again.

When I look back at the big picture of my life now, with the confidence of experience and success, I can easily see how Michael and "God" have always played a part in my life, and I can see with gratitude and humility the synchronicity of it all.

Jeff and I were married almost immediately, without any hesitation or doubt. We both knew the time was right. We didn't try to articulate the "whys." We had helped each other to bring out something special that had been closed off for many years. For me, that something was spirit.

Our families could not comprehend what had possessed us to marry at the spur of the moment on April Fool's Day in Las Vegas, Nevada. To say they were shocked would be an understatement. Neither of us were prone to such spontaneous commitments. In fact, my track record for dating before marriage had been excellent, the first time around.

Our marriage began with a new home, new cars, and all the other wonderful accouterments that accompany most marriages. However, we were also sharing something neither of us had ever experienced. We didn't give this new experience a name, but I always knew it was "God" within me, finally experiencing the fullness of marriage as I had always dreamed it to be.

Jeff never called his experience "God." For him, it was simply "a quiet, peaceful sense from within" that he had always possessed, only now he was sharing it with a partner. Jeff had the ability to stay centered during good times and bad. This was very new to me, as everyone I had known up to that point in my life had always been quick to react to bad times.

As Jeff and I moved along in marital bliss, we also had to contend with my Kirk and the battles that would spring up with him. Several people expressed their concern for my boys' welfare during their visits with Kirk. Jeff and I were aware of Kirk's habitual drug use, yet, we were trying to be fair and give him the benefit of the doubt: that he was capable of remaining sober and in control around the boys. We tried to convince ourselves that it was best for the boys to see their father, no matter the risk. It was only after Lisa (my sister) received an anonymous phone call that we changed our opinion as to his visitation rights.

The caller would not identify herself. She only said that she was the wife of someone who knew the boys' father very well and that the boys were in grave danger. Lisa listened to her and said that although she would pass the message on to me, this was something that I really had to hear for myself. The woman did not want to give her phone number, but she did agree to call me. I shortly thereafter received her call and once again she asked to remain anonymous. I told her I wasn't willing to honor her concerns for my boys if she wasn't willing to establish credibility with her name. She understood my situation and why she needed to reveal her name and because we knew a mutual friend trust was established.

Jeff and I confronted the bigger picture that we had tried so hard to ignore: Kirk's drug use was apparently overtaking his ability to see what was healthy and necessary for our son's, Jacob and Adam. This new reality was horrifying, for all the obvious reasons. The boys loved their father and I had to be the bad guy. After speaking with Jacob and Adam, Jeff and I found out many details about Kirk's neglect that they were feeling as well. Jeff and I made a decision to terminate the boys' visitation with their father until he could make a commitment to them, their well being, and his role as a father.

This decision did not come easy. Jeff and I knew we had to tell the boys everything that we had done in the past regarding our experimentation with drugs, in order for them to see how we *had made* a commitment to appropriately raising children. We strongly believed that we could not expose their father's use of drugs without being completely honest about our own past use. Incidentally, Kirk's drug use did not need to be exposed by us; it had already been revealed by his own negligence of being discreet about it during their visitations.

Neither Jeff nor I felt judgmental toward Kirk.

We believed that he had lost his perspective on the necessary priorities required in raising children. There was no way to juggle drugs, alcohol and children. At this time I needed "God" badly. I'd like to interrupt my own narrative to make the following point:

We all have times in our lives when we are given messages by what I call "spirit" to aid us in manifesting our heart's desire. If we choose to follow this guidance, our desires can be manifested without pain, struggle or fear. I call this our "Window of Opportunity." If we close our heart to our own message, it doesn't mean our desires won't eventually manifest, but the time and ease with which they will occur are altered. The obstacles Jeff and I went through with Kirk were the same ones Troy, the man I had dated after Kirk and before Jeff, had known we would have to face had we continued our relationship. Troy had loved me and my boys, and he had wanted to marry me, yet he had felt that he couldn't navigate the anger, violence, and hurt that Kirk was going to inevitably wreak upon us. Troy and I had therefore gone our separate ways after that fateful Valentine's Day, our paths rarely crossing thereafter.

However, during the many years following that breakup, through my commitment to spirit and my marriage to Jeff, many of our wounds were able to heal, and many of our obstacles were cleared. I didn't know this at the time, but I wasn't the only one processing and healing: Troy was also successful in his own healing.

It would be seven years after Troy and I had split, that our "Window of Opportunity" would come full circle, and "spoiler alert": this time we would be able to follow our messages, and to this day, I am happy to reveal that Troy and I remain happily married. But let's not get too far ahead of ourselves.

5

Meeting Michael

Over the course of many years, I had intuited on three separate occasions that my guardian angel was Archangel Michael. The first time I was reminded of Michael's presence was on a trip to Sedona, Arizona with my sister Lisa and her husband. At that time, I was separated, but not divorced from Kirk, and I was not dealing well with the situation. Lisa and her husband had therefore thought it would be good for me to get away.

We were wandering through the novelty shops in Sedona when we came across a lady reading Tarot cards. None of us believed in this sort of thing. In fact, we were laughing at the absurdity of even having her read my cards, just as some of you may be laughing at some of the passages in my story. However, Lisa and her husband encouraged me to give it a shot, for the mere entertainment of it all.

To our surprise, the woman was extremely accurate and told me many things that were true. She confirmed that I had been highly intuitive as a child, but that I had chosen to shut it off because of my fear of alienation and ridicule. She said that I was named after Archangel Michael (unbeknownst to her, my middle name is Michelle which is the feminine version of Michael) and that he was waiting for me. She matter of factly told me that all I needed to do was ask for his assistance, and he would be there. I paid the woman, took the audio cassette that came with my reading, and went on my way, occasionally reminiscing from time to time on what she had said, but not giving it any real attention.

The second incident occurred about a year later, when my friend Robert mentioned having gone to see a woman whom he knew to have accurate psychic abilities. At this time, I wasn't consciously aware of multi-sensory beings, but I knew I had a desire for something more than what ordinary life had to offer. I booked an appointment with this "psychic" woman, and she spoke to me of people in my life who had passed on, giving me their exact names, along with specific messages they had or me. Along with the messages of those from my past, she told me I had Archangel Michael at my side, and all I need do was ask for his guidance.

The third and final occasion, occurred when I began to work with an intuitive counselor who also mentioned the presence of an angel named Michael. The counselor didn't elaborate much, except to say that Michael was always with me. Despite the obvious coincidences of all three people's messages, each time I was told about Michael, it meant nothing to me. I took nothing to heart. I was busy living my life. At that point, anonymous phone calls and rumors were circulating about my ex-husband. A practical decision about those concerns needed to be made. My logical mind was telling me how important it was for boys to be with their biological father, even though my heart knew it was no longer safe for them to be around him.

One day, I found myself in the shower, devastated, confused, and hysterically crying, so I finally asked "God" to reveal to me anything that would help, including this Archangel Michael that I had been hearing so much about. If he really was here to help me, then "now was the time." I could no longer do it on my own. I would love to sound dramatic and claim that calling upon "God" to reveal Michael was a monumental scene with a divine light appearing in my shower stall, similar to Moses and the burning bush, but...

...That was not the case. I am a knowing-based person, which means I receive messages through an inner awareness. I didn't see, hear or feel his presence. I had an overwhelming awareness of his presence and I simply knew from that day forward that I was never going to be alone again. Awareness may not be what you think it is, so it's important to understand that Michael's presence was as real as any person I could have touched. My life was forever changed. My tea party companion had returned.

The wonderful truth is that I had never been without Michael. I was simply receiving his communication differently from when I was a little girl. Looking back, there were many occasions in which inexplicable coincidences had saved me.

One very clear "coincidence" was one I alluded to earlier in the book when my ex-husband, Kirk, was completely irrational and very drugged out. He had thrown me to the ground, gotten on top of me and started strangling me. Just before I was about to black out I felt Kirk being thrown off of me. He then ran to the bedroom, got his nine-millimeter pistol, came back to where I was standing, and I, having fully regained consciousness, saw him waving it around while screaming at me. That's when the police came to the door.

After taking him into custody the police officer told me they had received a call from our residence! This was an impossibility, as we had been the only ones at home and in the house. I suggested to the police that perhaps it had been a neighbor who had made the call, but the officer assured me that the call had been traced to our house and our number. Later, I was able to put together the strange and unexplained occurrences of that day.

The next few days were intense. I filed for divorce and we were scheduled to go to trial for my husband's assault on me. I didn't want to prosecute; I just wanted the divorce. The state, on the other hand, wanted to prosecute Kirk, so he went on trial. It was at the trial that I learned about guns and their "hairpin triggers." The slightest movement could have set Kirk's gun off, and apparently, the gun he had been pointing at me not only had one, but it had been cocked, loaded and ready to shoot. The state was using me as their only witness and wanted to know if I could tell them whether he had his finger on the trigger of the gun or the barrel? Apparently, this was the determining factor on whether or not they they could achieve a conviction. I honestly couldn't remember, so there was no conviction.

Oftentimes, I reflect upon upsetting occurrences, situations or coincidences that have manifested in my life in order to seek out hidden lessons or veiled truths. I realize now that not every human does this. Days later, upon his release and much to my amazement, Kirk blamed me for his gun being confiscated by the police. The lack of responsibility and awareness that he revealed by this accusation and the fact that he was unable to learn something positive from this event shocked me.

In that moment, I realized it had been Michael who had created the sensation of Kirk being pulled off of me while I was being strangled. It was also through Michael that the police had been called and judging by the prosecutor's description of the fragility of a hairpin trigger, it had also been through Michael's intervention that the gun had been kept from firing.

And another important aspect of this experience of chaos, is that I remember experiencing calmness in my heart, not fear. It had seemed so strange, at first, how safe I had felt in the face of what could have been my death. In retrospect, I now knew that what those three wise and wonderful "psychic" women had said was true: The presence of a "Michael," Archangel Michael, had always been around me, forever at work in my life. All I had to do was ask.

Fortunately, it didn't take my verbal acknowledgment of him to witness his presence. He had always been there, hearing my calls, only through my heart and not just my words.

6

Michael's Impact

Now that I had established that Michael's presence was with me, and better yet, had always been with me, you would think that life would reveal itself as Heaven on Earth. Oh, how I wish that were true! Instead, the trials and tribulations of establishing a communication with him were extremely difficult and revealed much about who I thought myself to be as a person. I had to get to know myself in a way that I had never known to exist.

Of course I asked the obvious question, "Why me?" To which Michael simply replied, "You were open and ready." At that time our communication was solitary and confidential. I had him all to myself and it felt incredible. I was sharing a bond that surpassed anything I have ever experienced in my life with anyone, even to this day. To be more precise, the difficulty I had in the beginning of our conversations was discriminating between Michael's communication to me and the "self-talk" of my logical mind. Fortunately, Michael helped me through this difficulty with various methods of awareness that were undeniably accurate and left no room for questions.

One time, for example, I was out to dinner with my family at a fast food restaurant when I was handed the receipt for our meal. I looked at the total and saw that it came to $16.16. At that moment Michael "told[1]" me to remember those numbers, so I made a mental note. Three days later, I received a letter from our mortgage company. We had sold our house a few months before and, in my mind, this letter could only be bad news. Much to my delight I found a refund check made out to us for $1,616.16! Instant shock set in, followed by jubilation at Michael's blatant display of his incredible role in my life.

Things weren't all fantastic, however. As Michael and I were forming our bond, Jeff was becoming skeptical of Michael's presence in my life and whether he indeed existed, and also whether or not the messages I had received from him were true. "Coincidence" was Jeff's strict diagnosis. I felt confronted and conflicted by his lack of faith. After all, he had seemed to have known and trusted my words and experiences when we had first gotten first together. Then again, my knowing certain things at that time had been labeled as "gut instinct" or "intuition" both explanations that Jeff could handle. Once I knew and acknowledged the name Archangel Michael as the source behind my intuitive gifts, the dynamics of our relationship forever shifted.

---

[1] As mentioned previously, Michael speaks through an awareness, and not a personified voice, but I will continue to use words like "said" and "told" to best relate my story as I continue.

Jeff desperately wanted to disprove my new allegiance with Michael. He asked me to call our mortgage company to verify that the check was real. The woman at the mortgage company also expressed how unusual the amount on the check was. Yet, after double-checking the figure, she verified its accuracy.

To this day I find myself in awe of the messages that the angels and spirit guides bring me. The only difference between my perspective and that of many others who hear my story is the fact that I quickly got to a point in my life where I could no longer question their authenticity.

I think most people who can recall their childhood would admit that there was a time when they trusted what we know to be our own truth. As children, our spirits are so much a part of "God" that we don't find it strange to see miracles all around us. It is usually only after we become aware of our human reality and its logic that we also become skeptical and sometimes even cynical about these many "obvious," little miracles.

And even though I now write with the confidence of years of direct experiences, I can easily remember a time, early on as an intuitive educator, when I lost sight of life's miracles. I have always experienced a lot of doubt from non-believers about my communication with Michael, other angels, spirit guides, and people who have passed over. People have often chosen to ridicule what they do not want to believe in, instead of accepting me as an intuitive educator. The weight of their accusations has often been daunting. Naturally, as I have continued the pursuit of my work and the challenges that accompany it, I have sometimes felt discouraged. In these early times in my career, Michael, to boost my morale, would ring my phone every night before I went to sleep. Amazingly, it was never at the same time since I would go to bed anywhere between 9:30 p.m. and midnight. It was just a quick "ring...ring," signaling to me that I was doing a good job and should not get discouraged. My deepest purpose is to assist others, and Michael has literally checked in on me to help me never waiver in this cause.

I have also communicated with other angels and spirits besides Michael. The feeling is best described as a vibration coming from inside my body. It is very intense, especially when dreaming. I feel a "thickness" around me, what I now know to be my etheric body.

When these experiences first occurred, they were very strange and frightening. I would see shadows of angels and spirits or small particle-like objects flashing and moving about, and in this transitional state I would be fully aware of my etheric reality, yet, always focused on the physical and human realm in which I was grounded. And if someone interrupted me, as in my tea party sessions, it would jolt me out of the experience and I would feel very exposed, vulnerable, and hypersensitive to my surroundings.

Most individuals experience the etheric realm while in their sleep. My first recollection of spending time in that reality was around the ages of five to seven. I would be deep into a dream or etheric state and would awaken to my parents calling my name and finding myself in the bedroom closet crying. I recall only the red painted shelves in my closet, the leftover Chinese red paint from our kitchen, and the feeling of being lost. One episode, the way my sister tells it, sent me into hysterics, scaring her so badly that she thought I was never going to come out of that "state." Lisa had been very scared, especially since she had heard somewhere to never wake a sleepwalker, for they could die of a heart attack.

So, as she stood at the door of our closet whispering my name, praying I'd snap out of it, I did, eventually, and then I proceeded back to bed as if nothing had happened. However, when Lisa later revealed her fear to me, it impacted me so greatly that my dreams no longer resulted in sleepwalking. It was fear I was feeling, while being awakened, that made me cry, the fear of not knowing where I was, like in the closet, or why I was there. I was receiving messages in my dream state and since I didn't know what they were and there wasn't anyone who could explain what was happening to me, I quite naturally became fearful.

I also remember as a child asking my parents to explain the dreams, vibrations, and flashes of light I had experienced, and their ensuing frustration at not knowing how to answer me. Michael said their inability to remember their own experiences of childhood resulted in frustration and perceived inadequacies as parents. Michael has since helped me to heal my fears and memories of the past, for which I am eternally grateful. Had these healings not taken place, I would not have been able to help my son through similar experiences.

My youngest son Adam is a visual intuit (meaning he receives his messages through visual images), and I remember when he was a child, he would sometimes come to me in the middle of the night in a frightened state or with a frozen stare. He was clearly seeing something that I wasn't seeing and trying to talk with me, though not conscious of me. He was frightened by the "things" he was seeing, things he couldn't describe.

And even though I had my own intuitive sensations and experiences, the truth is that I was scared! My faith in Michael was strong, but up until that point, I had only been dealing with my experiences and beliefs outside of the physical realm. I knew then and there that I had to let go of my fear and align myself with Michael. Once I centered myself, I was able to ask and receive a message from him as to what I needed to do.

Before bedtime that same evening, our family had been having a wonderful time playing with balloons in the living room. We had been throwing them into the air, seeing if we could keep them up off the ground. The "things" Adam was seeing later that evening were little "light beings" that wanted only to continue to play with him after he had gone to bed. My first responsibility was to let go of my fear, realign with my truth, see the situation for what it truly was, and then help Adam through it all so he could alleviate his fears and find his own truth. This turned out to be an uncomplicated process of simply and gently calling Adam back to this earthly reality.

I believe each generation takes their memories and beliefs of "God" to a higher level than the generation that preceded them. I had done so much work on clearing away my old wounds by this time that it was much easier for me to help Adam than it had been for my own parents to help me.

7

Eye of the Storm

There is only one thing that stands in the way of knowing, feeling, or sensing our connection to "God"; It is our strong right and wrong judgment that we direct toward others and ourselves. If we stop the doubting process that throws us out of this divine connection, we need nothing else. Most of us spend our waking hours trying to connect to people, situations or things that we believe, on some level, will help us feel peace, harmony, and contentment in our heart.

The truth is that any connection to something other than "God" is a momentary "fix," usually lasting only until the next crisis, or, metaphorically speaking, until the next two-by-four to the head or tornado impacts our lives and throws us into panic and fear. The solution to crisis is to ask for guidance when we feel ourselves combating outside forces and to stop giving them more validity than the inner peace that "God" provides.

Gratefully, I grew up commonly drawing upon this guidance while living with my parents and then, after the divorce and my marriage to Jeff, I was given a very valuable lesson that Kirk generously provided.

One afternoon, Jeff and I were inside the house, getting ready to take the boys out to dinner, but as the boys waited for Jeff and I in the front yard, Kirk and his new wife drove by on his Harley Davidson. Upon seeing the boys alone, they decided to pull up in front of the house to speak with them, despite a clear court order forbidding him to do so.

By this time, the boys had witnessed enough incidents of abuse that they did not welcome the possibility of interacting with their father's hostility again. So, when Kirk called Jacob over, Jacob stood frozen in his tracks.

It was at this moment that I walked out to see the mixture of love and confusion on Jacob's face. I quietly asked Jacob to step back and attempted to speak to Kirk with the hopes of diffusing any confrontation. I explained that the boys needed continuity, and that if he wanted to begin seeing them again, we would need to go through the court system. He called me a few choice names, gathered a large amount of spit into his mouth and spat it directly into my face and hair. He then took off, just as Jeff and my father walked out of the house.

I was mortified, humiliated, and frankly down- right shocked at what he had done. The man I had married, my high school sweet heart, was no longer behind the eyes of the man that had spit in my face. There wasn't a trace of him left that I could see. At first, I was furious. After all, despite years of trying to work things out with him and turning the other cheek when he didn't pay his child support or keep his obligations to the boys, he was still hostile and vengeful toward me—continuing to blame me for his shortcomings.

In the years after we divorced, Kirk had been delinquent in his child support payments, at that time owing $5,900. Fed up, I made a phone call, and he was picked up and put into jail for a few days until he was able to borrow the money for his release. I didn't like the fact that it was the result of my call that he was there; however, I also had to support my children.

After this incident, things definitely weren't good between us, yet somewhere along the way we managed to become civil, but when he again got behind on his payments, I scheduled a court date. I picked him up to take him to the court, and once we were in front of the judge, I asked that the new total of $6,700 due the boys be forgiven, his child support reduced, and that he be given another chance to succeed as a father. The judge made me repeat, then and there, that I understood in forgiving the past amount, I could not, in the future, go after it; that it was completely erased from the records as delinquent and owed. I acknowledged that I did, indeed, understand. Kirk and I went to lunch after court that day, and it felt like we had both found a remembrance of why we had married so many years before.

But at the time of the spitting incident, I had somehow forgotten about all the negative energy churning inside of him and the fact that I had *always* been the safest target for its release. Had I remembered that, his treatment of me in front of my parents' house would not have been so surprising! After he spat on me, when I finally calmed down, I asked Michael what it had been all about. He told me, "When you get too close to a lion that hasn't been fed, he will strike out."

I then understood some of what Kirk was going through. He had not had the best childhood and had never healed the wounds from his bad relationship with his father. Therefore, he had no idea what to do for his own children.

Although this did not mean I was going to subject my children to any more of their father's destructive behavior, I did come to a place where my love for his soul had returned. I felt empathy for his wounded spirit in a way I had never before experienced. No longer did I judge why he wasn't the father we wanted him to be. He simply wasn't yet willing to heal himself.

The "lion" Michael was referring to, that hadn't been fed, was his soul. He was still abusing drugs, trying to survive, and his spirit was void of self-love.

No one could give Kirk love because he did not love himself. It reaffirmed that my boys and I could not be in physical contact with him, but it also made it clear that we could and should not condemn or judge him. We would have to love his soul forever — praying that someday he would awaken to his true "God Self."

This was a valuable lesson. Yet, teaching my children to love his soul as well as helping them to understand their own boundaries was not an easy task. "God," giving the boys a wonderful dad in Jeff, to physically love them and be there for them in ways their biological father couldn't, did not have to detract from the love they felt for their dad, nor the love he felt for them. My boys are extraordinary young men. Given the extreme circumstances of their childhood, the work they have done for themselves and the spiritual beings that they show themselves to be, every single day, is honorable. They dealt with a lot of turmoil in their young lives and have become stronger for it.

Another blessing from that moment was that saw in Jeff a calmness that wasn't always present in my life. I had never met a man who could stay centered in the midst of his wife going through such turmoil and not get angry or want retaliation. It was a gift watching him stay centered during the many bad times, always knowing what to do without letting his ego take over to rule the kingdom of hatred. Jeff was a magnificent teacher of self-love. The stability of his soul wasn't shaken by worldly affairs.

This incident's impact on me also affected my interactions with family and clients. My world has been enriched by the experience. The challenges I was given in dealing with my ex-husband gave me the ability to step beyond judgment what, in the past, had seemed justifiable. Kirk gave me many reasons to feel justified in being right and in judging his behavior, yet, "God" gave me wisdom that has far exceeded any rationale to condemn him.

When I first wrote this book, the story of Kirk and my family was not complete; sadly, a few years after the first edition publication of this book, Kirk was killed in a drug-related shooting. Looking back, I can now see why I was faced with such devastating challenges. Though the pain can never be erased, my boys and I took the pain of our experiences and chose to heal. Through spiritual guidance, we accepted the man Kirk had become and in the wake of his death, we grieved for the husband and father he had once been. Jacob, Adam, and I were truly blessed to have been given and met those challenges in learning how to not judge before his death, for we were able to say goodbye to Kirk with love, cherished memories, and open hearts.

8

Who Are We?

In the beginning of our spiritual journey we experience difficulty in remembering how to connect to "God." However, once our memory is properly jogged, connection becomes second nature. Finally, toward the end of our quest of learning, we remember "who we are" as a Divine Connection to "God Eternal"; but even this can create difficulties. Because of the euphoria of our return to our higher selves, we can have difficulty staying connected or grounded in the reality of human consciousness. Human consciousness seems chaotic when compared to Divine Connection, so often our natural response is to lift out of the human reality. This can sometimes feels as though you are losing touch with reality or going "insane." Some people at this last stage of remembering "who we are" actually give up and become ungrounded. I experienced this pull within myself.

My best conversations with Michael occur in the early morning hours when I first awaken for the new day. I lay in bed with my eyes closed and converse anywhere from 15 minutes to a couple of hours, depending on what Michael has to impart to me for that day. I cherish this time.

On one occasion, I had been having a challenging week. It was nothing specific, just challenging. One morning that week, I awoke to darkness. Not only was the room dark, but my soul felt dark. I thought Satan had taken me over, which seems like a very insane thought, especially because I don't actually believe Satan is anything more than our own darkness or negative thoughts.

Despite my "normal" philosophy, all of a sudden, "Satan" was real! I had had an interaction with a client earlier that week, which I will relate in full detail later, and while in bed, I had a very dark thought, for a brief moment, *Maybe he was right; maybe I am Satan!*

I lay in bed stricken with morose thoughts of my death, of nothingness, and of slipping into an insanity from which I would never return. I was paralyzed with fear. I reached for the phone and called Lisa who, luckily for me, lived next door. Lisa came over and sat on my bed, holding my foot. She didn't say anything profound. She just sat with me — helping me to balance and ground myself.

I do not subscribe to any one religion, but I do recognize wisdom in all its forms. So, as Jesus once said, when you are clear with "who you are," you must, choose, "to be in the world but not of it." This choice seems to be a simple one.

However, when you are the one making the choice, it is not so easy. The world does not really offer a great deal to those who have reached a point of self-awareness and clarity, except to be of service to "God." This feeling is not always pleasant, for it poses a challenge of staying centered and not getting sucked into human drama.

It is very important to mention that the choice is always ours to either stand in the "eye of the hurricane" where it's calm, or to remain in the chaos. "God" gave us this choice by giving us free will to choose him or not to choose him.

Remember, there is no right or wrong because we are only here to learn from our life experiences in order to remember "who we are," and undoubtedly, "who we are" is the part of life that feels the most difficult. No matter what judgments we make upon others or ourselves, we cannot, in the long run, forget "who we are."

There is always a part of us that does not understand exactly what is necessary to move us forward. Yet, if you continually reconnect yourself to "God," there will always be the truth at the conclusion of our struggles in life. Remain open for all experiences in order to give yourself the entire truth, and allow yourself to experience the fullness of what "God" has in store for you. I want to reiterate that this strategy can sometimes feel very disconcerting, especially if we are standing in the way of our own abundance from "God." But, the truth is simple: we always have the ability to step aside and receive the goodness from "God." However, most of us don't believe it can be that simple.

Something I have learned well is that the common mistake that many of us make is in thinking that "what we do" is "who we are." This is far, so far, from the truth. Yet, it is a form of mistaken identity that we must all go through before fully understanding our purpose in life. "Who we are" is the gas station attendant, the business owner or the preacher who understands that what he or she does to earn a living is not who he or she is. When we understand "who we are," we experience the peace, love, and joy coming from him or her every time we come in contact with that person.

Conversely, we have also experienced the gas station attendant, the business owner, or the preacher who thinks that what he or she does is who he or she is and with these people, we experience judgment, lack of joy, non-fulfillment, and ego instead of peace, love, and joy. "Who we are" is a divine connection to "God" and remembering that divine connection is merely a matter of when.

We each will find our way, and once we get to this level, we will begin the process of determining what would be the most beneficial service to "God," to ourselves, and to others in the most expansive way possible. Most likely, you will go through many tests to determine what "God's will" looks like, and in the process, you will weed out many things you thought were your "gifts" to impart to the world. Also, you may find many of your gifts were just tools for meandering the road to getting you to your purpose. It matters not what you do with who you are as long as it serves "God," yourself, and others in the greatest possible way.

Some people think they must have high spiritual status in order to serve "God," but this isn't true at all. It matters not what we do; only that we stay grounded in who we are while we are doing it. This is the trick to staying centered while the world's human consciousness tries to pull you out of alignment with your purpose. There isn't anything wrong with human consciousness; going in and out of it is normal. It's getting stuck in it that causes disharmony.

Serving "God" is a remarkable experience, whether you are caring for children, running a nation, bagging groceries, or helping people on their spiritual journey, as I have been guided and have chosen to do. Once you know "who you are," what you do with that will simply be the greatest expansion of "God" for you.

9

The Gift of Detachment

In returning to our heart connection, we will process many past memories, experiences, and les- sons—whatever is needed to get there. We need to allow ourselves the freedom to know that we all get thrown off course from time to time and sucked into our human consciousness, our logical mind. This is not "bad." We merely need to ask the question, "Does this serve me?" Staying centered consists of continuously being aware of what is happening within your inner-self and asking yourself if you are experiencing "the calm."

This calm to which I refer isn't necessarily a "feel good" kind of place. In the midst of life's madness, we all have felt a certain calm that we sometimes may have experienced as happiness, discomfort, or even sadness. Yet, always present is peace, tranquility, or "calm," and we know, without fail, in what direction to proceed to move forward in our life.

Early on, while still working full time and only contemplating the "fantasy" of doing intuitive consulting as a profession, my niece Marley, Lisa's daughter, became very ill with a temperature of 103 degrees. At the time, Marley was only seven months old. She was burning with a fever, yet very coherent and even happy, as though nothing was amiss.

Normally, any mother would call a doctor first thing if her child had such a fever, yet Lisa got the message to call me and work through whatever was causing Marley's illness. I asked Michael, and got the message that Marley didn't need to go to the doctor. She was clearing away impurities and would be fine after a cool bath. Lisa bathed her and Marley cooled down for about an hour or so. Then, Lisa called again saying her temperature was now at an often-fatal 105 degrees.

I again asked what needed to be done, and Michael told me that Lisa needed to take her outside in the fresh air, rub her down with ice, and pull the energy from her. All the while, as I was relaying this message, my logical mind kept getting in the way saying, *But, maybe you should take her in to the doctor, too.* After all, this was my sweet little niece, and I didn't want to be wrong and have anything happen to her.

Lisa was strong, however. She stayed centered throughout the experience, telling me that she trusted my messages and that, if and when a time came that she knew she had to take her to the doctor, she would do so. She took Marley outside, gave her a rub down, and pulled out the energy. Within 20 minutes, Marley's temperature was back to normal. Lisa and I stayed in the "calm," even though it didn't feel "good," and we detached ourselves from the fears of Marley's situation.

Do I give this message to anyone calling me for medical input? Absolutely not. In every individual case, I listen to my message and pass it along. It is the responsibility of those coming to me to discern for themselves what to do with my messages. During Marley's crisis, Lisa's confidence in my intuitive abilities, as well as her own, moved us through the attachment to what stops us on an intellectual level from entering into our connection with "God" and allowing for "miracles" to emanate when trusting the "God" within us.

In different moments of my life, I have stopped myself from going forward with my work, out of fear of what might happen if someone followed one of my messages and something terrible were to happen.

During one such moment of doubt, Michael reminded me of a time when I had to meet with Jacob's teacher and was told that Jacob should go on Ritalin to help him with his school studies.

I neither condemn nor condone taking medication. Rather, I knew, as Jacob and I had discussed previously, that this was not the route he wanted to take. Jacob had said that he wanted to get good grades, but he didn't want the effects that the medication would have on his life, outside of bettering his school grades.

So after we yet again discussed the teacher's advice, Jacob and I sat down and discussed what it would take for him to make good grades and made a plan for organization at home as well as at school, such as setting him up with tutoring, etc. We took responsibility for the message the teacher had given us about the medication and used our own discernment as to what to do with it.

A while later, when it was conference time again, I met with his teachers, and every one of them commended both Jacob and I on our commitment to school. He was making the same passing marks as students that were on medication, only he was not taking any. The teacher was responsible in relaying his message about the medication, but I was responsible in my response to it.

The occasional doubts about something terrible happening to my clients no longer exists. Michael has reminded me enough times that my only responsibility is to staying in alignment and receiving and relaying accurate messages without adding my own interpretations. This is where a lot of people tend to foul themselves up, by making their own interpretations as opposed to keeping the message's wisdom clear and concise. The "calm" is the centered connection to our "God Consciousness."

Unfortunately, most of us act with a human consciousness that drives us to remain attached to our human emotions, feelings, and actions. My intent is not to connote our human consciousness with negativity, but only to point out that it serves as a connection to the Earth plane and to other individuals on a physical level.

Attachment, just as Buddhism relates, is the thing that throws us into judgment of others and ourselves. When we get attached to someone, something, or some situation, we begin the process of falling out of connection with "God"; our attachment takes us out of our "center." I now find a certain amusement when I see my attachments pop up. But that hasn't always been the case.

For my 32nd birthday, I was taken to an expensive steakhouse to celebrate. While I was enjoying my filet mignon (I love filet mignon), I got a message from Michael, loud and clear, to enjoy my steak because, after this meal, I would become a vegetarian. Needless to say, my instant reaction to this was, I don't think so!

Adamantly, I dug my heels in and wanted to know why? His reply was simple. I needed to lighten the vibration of my energy in order to handle the intense work upon which I was about to embark. I will readily admit that my attitude with Michael has oftentimes been one of "Do I have to?" which is much like that of a child pleading with his or her parents not to make him or her do homework, even though they know it will bring good grades.

Knowing Michael would never request anything unnecessary for my spiritual growth and well being, I have dutifully listened and followed through with his message. At that time, I assumed that my vegetarian status would last forever. Fortunately for me, as abruptly as he came to me with the message to quit eating meat, he also came to me 18 months later with the message that I could integrate meat back into my diet with poultry and fish first, then, if I desired, other meats.

Was he kidding? Of course I desired this! In making the choice to detach from my perceived agony of what his request would cost me, I found that following his direction was easier than I could imagine when not engaged in my drama.

Attachment comes in all forms. Many challenges have come to me through relationships with friends and family. My commitment to the integrity of my chosen work often calls for me to be brutally honest, and several close friendships have suffered because of this. Most of my friendships from the past contained a lot of what I call "fluff." I define "fluff" as conversations filled with what sounds nice, or what we want to hear, avoiding subjects and decisions that bring pain or sadness, deflecting truth, which could move us forward. Fluff is neither good nor bad. It is just something I have found I had to dispense with so I could start speaking my truth.

I have come to understand that the mere stuffing of emotions causes us to put unnecessary amounts of energy into being unauthentic. I can sense when something is out of alignment just by being present with people. The honesty I bring into my relationships, whether with family or friends, I ask for in return. It may not always be easy or fun to be in a relationship with me. However, the dedication it brings to our lives is always rewarding.

For many years, especially during my high school years, I chose to shut down this part of my intuition so I could hold back any comments that could be confrontational and cause someone to dislike me. The amount of energy it took to stop myself from speaking what was in my heart was enormous; and, in doing so, I stored it in my logical mind, resulting in judgment of myself. There were so many times when I consciously remained silent, choosing to say nothing, resulting in a superficial relationship with a friend, as opposed to speaking my truth, all for fear of losing friendship.

When I began to look at my own life and the issues in it, I realized that replaying all my stories of pain and hurt had never served me, and I was going to have to go deep to heal them. The same became true for me in many of my friendships. Friends would come to me for advice, rehashing old wounds time and again, wanting my help, yet shutting down when I told them what they did not want to hear..

It came to the point when I had to let some of these friendships go. I didn't want to hurt these people with truths about issues I could see, while they were unwilling to see them. I chose to release these friendships rather than shut myself down. Many friends thought I was judging them and the attachment I felt of no longer physically having them in my life was a price I was willing to pay in order to be true to myself.

I knew that our hearts would share a love for the past, present, and future, whether or not our paths ever crossed again. After some time, those willing to look deeper into the truth understood that I was simply pointing out a wound that needed attention so they could heal it and step fully into their hearts. Those friendships have become stronger.

Friends were not the only people I had to release. I also had clients who believed my discernment was judgment. Michael's energy is quite intense, and the bluntness in which it is sometimes delivered does not always work for certain clients. I begin my relationships, whether it be with a client, friend or family member, by letting the person know that the method in which I align with Michael is one of climbing straight up the mountain as opposed to gradually ascending the mountain on switchbacks. Neither method is right or wrong. It is simply the way my energy with Michael is used.

For many years, people have said to me, "You are so intense," and I used to cringe as if I had just been called a horrible name. I have detached the emotions that I previously tied to the word "intense" and now embrace the fact that this is the way I am, without apology or excuses. Michael's energy is intense, hence my intensity. As I have said, my work with Michael does not work for everyone. Letting go of people that choose a different path, however difficult, is essential if I am to remain authentic to "God" and myself.

When we are born, we live completely in our heart space until we are taught logic. Unfortunately, most of us go from connecting to our heart to connecting to our logic or ego instead of learning to balance the two. Many of us have been living in our logical mind in order to survive childhood wounds and circumstances. We do not comprehend that with the mind, or logic, come emotions.

We think that emotion is a function of the heart and therefore do not proceed with the messages we are given by "God" and our spirit guides for fear of the pain. Our mind is what connects emotions to our memories of the past. Our heart is what is connected to "God," and "God" is here to help us remember Him, not to harm us to the point of forgetfulness.

Attachment can also come in the form of detachment. To become completely detached from the world can also be detrimental. I spoke of the incident in which my ex-husband Kirk spat in my face and then took off upon seeing Jeff and my father. I remember thinking how wonderful it was that I had a husband that didn't react to Kirk's hatred, and in fact, I *am* fortunate to have had that.

However, what I realized later was the harmful extent to which he didn't react. Emotions run very high in my family; whether it is happiness, sadness, grief, or anger, and especially anger. When expressed, these emotions are expressed very passionately. When expressed in the negative, they can be very frightening, and when expressed positively, they are jubilant.

My father is half-Lebanese and half-Irish, both very passionate cultures. They manifest themselves both positively and negatively. My father's first instinct is to avenge the family name. So, you can imagine how protective he became when he saw that I had been spit upon. Jeff, on the other hand, stayed very calm throughout the whole ordeal. Like I said, I was thankful the situation didn't get volatile, and that we were able to deal with the matter appropriately, through the court system.

Later, however, I realized the degree to which Jeff had been emotionally unaffected. I wasn't looking for him to go after my ex-husband with a baseball bat, yet, there was an absence of empathy or compassion for what his wife and sons had just experienced. There seemed to be no depth of concern in his communication with others and myself about it. Jeff had detached from expressing all emotion. Given the background I had come from, this response, which at first seemed refreshing, at that time appeared as an unwillingness to relate.

10

Evil or Darkness

I do not believe there is anything that possesses a power greater than "God." Thus, believing that something other than "God" has any power over us does and should not exist. That is not to say that so-called evil or dark energy does not exist. It simply does not have any power over light or "God." When you live this concept, you will no longer believe in darkness or evil forces having power over you. You will merely stand in the light and the darkness will cease to be.

This negative energy has many names: Satan, darkness, the Devil, evil, etc. Whatever label you use, it has absolutely no power over "God," Universal Energy or Light. I refer to this negative energy as "lower-level consciousness." Many people live in various degrees of consciousness from extreme lows to enlightened highs. Only humans can give this energy any power by acknowledging it as real. I am not saying it is not there nor very real to some people. However, when it is given energy on any level through fearing, it gains power in your life. When working with clients, I simply acknowledge the energy it's being given and put my full attention on "God," goodness, and light. When people are living in a lower-level consciousness, I refer to this as "Hell on Earth." Fear, in and of itself, is a precursor to this painful state of living. Individuals experiencing fear are not experiencing the presence of "God." The Universe is always waiting for us to connect or align with ourselves. Yet our ability to exercise our right to free will sometimes throws us out of that alignment.

"God" is the only power. Therefore, anything opposing "God" falls into the category of fear. I am not referring to the fear we experience before doing something that we "know" is divinely guided such as jumping off of a high dive to face the fear of heights. The fear I am referring to is the one that literally separates you from "God." You know the difference because one will give you a pleasantly anxious or exciting feeling as you continue to stand in the "calm" place in your heart whereas the other will cause great questioning and doubt, in the deepest aspects of yourself, for everything that comes your way. I had a situation when I needed to face my own truth about "good" and "evil" early on in my professional intuitive work. I had been working pretty steadily with a client on transforming his dark energy into light. He was extremely intuitive, yet he could get swallowed up in his "darkness" or the aspects of himself that he feared to examine prior to our sessions.

He liked to express himself through his body, via, kick boxing and karate. Though I can appreciate this form of expression, his intentions or reasons behind these hobbies would bring energy that wasn't always alignment with his better self. Sparring must be done with the correct intentions of the heart. Otherwise, it simply becomes an outlet for aggressive, unresolved issues to emerge. We had worked through clearing many of his old issues that were out of alignment with his heart, and we had resolved much of the anger that resided deep within him. We had worked together regularly until he thought he could manage on his own.

He returned to me quite some time later, with a black cloud hovering above him. He had fallen out of alignment and the "demons," as he referred to them, were running rampant around him once again. The continued dedication to looking deep within himself and working diligently on his alignment with "God" was essential to his living peacefully, but he had not been doing this. He informed me that he had been to see a Shaman to help him release these so-called "demons," and the Shaman had sent him away.

My first reaction was also to send him away. After all, if a Shaman feared his energy, who was I to think I could help him? I asked Michael if there was anything I could do to help. The answer was, "Yes." He explained to me that what the Shaman did in sending him away was the right thing to do since that Shamanistic culture believed as much in the dark as the light, and through this they learn many great lessons from both. Being that my truth, or belief system, holds power only for the light, I was able to dispel the "demons" or darkness which the client had come in contact with, and he was able to once again hold his own light. I had to conquer my own logical fears that the darkness had any power over me.

Another eye-opening learning experience for me was with a client I had been working with for several months;

I mentioned him earlier in a reference to his thinking I was Satan. We had met while working at the same company. At that time, I was doing intuitive work, but only part-time. I didn't know this person on a personal level at all when Michael told me to go to him with a message. I didn't want to. I shared my connection to Michael with a lot of people who knew me and with whom I had some kind of credibility. However, exposing myself to a virtual stranger was more than I was willing to do.

Eventually, Michael's persistence won out, and as frightening as it was, I gave this acquaintance the message. We ended up talking for over an hour. When I left that company to do intuitive consulting full-time, this man became a client. I came to honor this man, his position in management at my former company, and his position at his church. Although his church did not believe in speaking with people who had passed on (angels and the like), this man recognized that my connection to Michael was as true as the connection he was experiencing with his own spirit guide. He and I both learned and grew a lot as a result of our sessions.

Approximately eight months later, after quite a number of sessions, he showed up for an appointment, but I was very surprised by the person who appeared before me. The man that showed up was not the man I had been having many heart to heart interactions with, but a man of the mind and not of the heart. He had come to the path in his journey of remembering who he was, when, his ego or human consciousness had stepped in and tried to erase his memory of the path that led to "God." I will never forget that day. He was so full of fear. He shortly thereafter accused me of following Satan! I was devastated. I felt betrayed by his about face and his lack of trust. How could he actually be thinking I was following the Devil? I felt myself losing center and giving him my power. I then remembered that Michael was with me, and I allowed Michael to carry me through the experience.

This client was so close to his truth and although I knew that he could live in his truth and in the truth of his church, although they appeared contrary, he did not believe this and therefore made the issue about me. At that point in the session, we could have ended our business relationship, being at odds with each other, but we did not. I stayed centered, and he again found his heart. That turned out to be our last session and, as uncomfortable as it was, we completed our time together with love in our hearts and respect for each other's truths.

I have found that in embracing both sides of "God," be it darkness or light, we will all at some point have to deal with the parts of us that we believe are evil or bad. This was my test. I found myself much stronger after these experiences. However, while dealing with them, it of course appeared to be more of a challenge than I bargained for. Michael did not agree. It provides testimony to the old adage that "God" never gives you more than you can handle.

11

Judgment Vs. Discernment

Discernment is a very tricky word. The dictionary defines it as, "The quality of being able to grasp and comprehend what is obscure; to detect with the eyes or senses; to understand the difference." I use this ability constantly in my work. In fact, it is imperative for me to have this ability in order to help those with whom I am working. Many people tend to misinterpret this ability as judgment. Make no mistakes; discernment does resemble judgment in certain situations. However, the meaningful differences between the two words are very distinct.

Using discernment is what gives me the ability to detect whether someone is in the "hurricane" or the "eye of the hurricane." In my field, this is extremely important in order to "know" exactly how to proceed with a session or interaction with a person. If the person I am working or interacting with is in the "darkness or lower level of consciousness," I must be aware of this, so that I may give it no energy and hold strong in my commitment to "God."

Without discernment, humans are susceptible to negative energy, especially, and ironically, through compassionate help. This is not to say that you must not use compassion and love in helping someone. However, you must not allow yourself to be tricked by their energy. This is where the distinction between judgment and discernment comes in. Judgment is the act of separating yourself from the other person and discernment is simply acknowledging their position and staying in a state of love and compassion.

Listening to our messages, once we receive them, is also crucial in determining how to proceed. There are four ways in which we receive our messages from Spirit: Knowing, Seeing, Feeling and Hearing. Everyone has a circuit in which Spirit talks to them through their intuition.

This circuit is much like that of a parent waking their child for school. Usually the child knows it is time to awaken. However, if they do not listen, then, that brings about the second message of their parent entering the room in a physical fashion, perhaps standing over them so they may see them. If that still does not awaken them, there may come a resounding touch or feeling and, of course, lastly, a sharp voice that they hear that will, if all else fails, awaken the sleeping child. "God" speaks to us in somewhat the same fashion through our intuition. My experience is that when I listen to "God" through my knowing and do not doubt or choose to ignore the message, this will suffice. However, many times I have fallen into doubt or literally chosen not to listen because I did not like the message I was receiving.

When I have done this, I have next experienced the same message through my visual senses; if I ignore this second version of the same message, this process will continue until all circuits have been used to get the message across. This is much like how parents, attempt to communicate with their children. It is much more pleasant, for both parties, to get the message the first time.

Let me give you an example of using discernment. Let's say you decide to dye your hair a completely different color from your natural coloring. The hairdresser will ask what your original color is, not to judge whether your hair is indeed the color you say, but to discern exactly what colors are needed to mix for the intended result. If you say you are blonde but your roots clearly show brunette, the result of the dye will be horrendous for you, your hair, and your hairdresser, because in taking your word, he or she will have judged what you said instead of using discernment and using what they would have known was the correct dye to use. This concept leads to one of many circumstances that I have had regarding discernment. Many people who are on the path of spiritual awakening, even though they have come to me as a client, willing to heal their spiritual pains, are too frightened or ashamed to bring up their issues because they feel I may judge them as "wrong" or "bad." If I operated in my logical mind, I most likely, would hold some sort of judgment regarding what they have done. However, Michael always gives me the truth of their heart so that I know exactly what path to take to best serve in healing their issue. When your heart is engaged, it is impossible to judge anything.

I started my professional career working with a client who quickly became a dear friend. At the time, it was a sticky situation, even with discernment. In one particular session, the lines between friendship and client were somewhat unclear and I was accused of stifling her spiritual growth. Intuitively, she knew that she would be doing work in the field of spirituality using her intuition. She felt that the time had come.

Michael very clearly told me that she needed more time for growth and to build confidence in herself and that she was not yet ready to move forward in that direction. I relayed the message I had been given, and although I knew it came from a place of discernment, she misinterpreted it as my judging her intuitive abilities.

I became the accused. She believed my intent was to hold her down and keep her from being an equal. I did, indeed, know she would be doing intuitive work, only in what vein I was not sure. Yet, had I encouraged her to take that step at that time in her life, it would have been devastating to her, emotionally, mentally, and physically.

I left the session swirling with anger from my sense of betrayal. After all, I was simply doing what I had been guided to do—to help people develop their intuitive abilities while ensuring their personal safety at the same time. I knew then that our friendship, at least for the time being, had come to an end.

It was difficult and uncomfortable to stay committed to my Higher Consciousness when it appeared that I was losing dear friends, and at this time, a moment of doubt again crept into me. I questioned if perhaps I was truly judging or if what my friend and client had said held any truth, for I know anger is a reaction to judgment, and I was indeed angry. What I realized was that the truth to be was not anger at my friend for the accusation, it was anger at Michael for putting me in a position in which I had to be the one to tell her to slow down.

I have had many exhausting conversations with Michael regarding my commitment to "God" and how to serve him in this capacity. I have come to understand why this incident with that client was a crucial lesson I needed to learn from. Without proper discernment, any action or thought can be disastrous to a person as well as those with whom he or she comes in contact with. Michael helped me to clearly understand the distinction between discernment and judgment as well as the importance of releasing attachment to other people's behaviors. The lessons here were invaluable, yet, they did, in the very least, cost me that friendship for quite some time.

The blessing behind what appears to be disappointment, anguish and sadness is the miraculous gifts that follow. Eight months after this incident, my friend called me and we worked through all that had transpired between us. Our friendship became stronger through this experience. She has since worked diligently on herself through various healers, successfully healing hurt people and fulfilling her heart and life purpose.

She has, indeed, found her calling through spiritual healing. Although the methods with which we approach our gifts of healing are different, I didn't allow her to rush herself into the process, and she has thus been ready and continues to be well prepared to handle anything that comes her way.

12

Victims — There Are None

We are responsible only for ourselves—our words, deeds, and actions. We have responsibilities, but we are responsible for only ourselves. When you make yourself responsible for anyone other than yourself, a mentality of fear says something outside of yourself has made this choice without your consent. We all possess the ability to be powerful beings. If you believe to any extent that someone or something outside of you can do anything that is out of your control, then, you have forfeited your power of connection to that belief and not to "God."

This forfeit of self happens so often, and in so many ways. Examples of this are when you give someone the right to ruin your day by cutting you off in traffic, struggle with an argument before leaving for work or school in the morning, or sense someone else's negative energy and mistakenly take it into yourself.

Of course, this includes even the big things in our lives such as divorce, sexual assault, robbery and murder. These are just a few examples of events that can occur which can immediately cause us to lose our connection or "power" to "God." The mere act of doing this starts the process of being the victim.

I am not saying that perpetrators of crimes should not be held accountable for their actions. However, to claim that you are powerless over these circumstances in your life creates the false authorship of becoming a victim. You always have a choice to use these experiences to grow, which leads to a much fuller experience of life. To be a victim stops this crucial process of growth.

I learned at the age of seven that life was more complicated than I had originally thought it was. It started with car rides with my grandfather. My dad's biological father died when he was fourteen from a heart attack. My grandma remarried later, and they moved to Phoenix where my family had settled. Grandpa Ken was thus the only grandfather I ever knew. Lisa and I justified the things he did to us as being not so bad because he wasn't our "real" grandpa. Somehow calling him "step-grandpa" made it all seem easier.

Ken would pick me up in his 1964 beige Cadillac while my grandmother waited for us at the house. "It" would only occur when my sister was not along for the ride. At the time I didn't know "it" was happening to her, too. He began fondling me whenever we were alone or if we were at his house and my grandma was in the back room ironing or napping.

The strangest part of it was that neither he nor I said a word. It was as if it wasn't really happening—it occurred in dead silence. My thoughts would run rampant, *What is he doing?* This is wrong! What do I do? I'm scared." However, I said nothing to anyone about what was happening. Ken never threatened me or told me not to tell my parents or Grandma. It was just understood that I was to say nothing. I closed off a portion of my heart, becoming numb and somehow putting myself into a trance until it was over. Although he was physically molesting me, he never hurt me physically, which is to say, we never had intercourse.

This experience continued sporadically until I was about eleven years old. By this time my sister and I knew Grandpa was "playing," as he referred to it, with both of us. Whenever we were to spend the night at my grandparents, we would come up with reasons not to go over there. But if we nevertheless had to go, we would stay close to our grandma so we didn't have to be alone with Ken. This method seemed to work as the incidents became fewer and further between until they just faded away. That is until one day when my parents went out of town.

My grandparents came to the house to watch us, and I had a friend stay the night. Grandpa Ken tried to molest my friend. I was devastated. When she told me what had happened, I thought I died inside. My heart was so hurt. I thought this was a thing of the past. How dare he humiliate me in front of one of my friends? I was livid inside and horribly embarrassed. I had handled the issues I had with my grandpa, so I was no longer his victim, but now he had, once again, crossed the line.

In trying to impose his sickness onto my friend, I felt hatred and disgust for him all over again. It was as though I had put it behind me and he brought it right back to the surface. I told my sister about what had happened and for the first time we went to our parents and told them what he had been doing to us over the years. It's funny how we often value others more than ourselves and are thus more willing to speak up when we see them being "victimized" than we are willing to when we experience it for ourselves.

My parents took care of the situation, and although it wasn't until years later that we were given details as to how they resolved it, we were instructed by our parents never to go near Grandpa Ken again. Ken remained a figure in our lives, but an adult was always present when he was around. My parents did not make him pay for his crime by putting him behind bars, but he did face consequences. All that we appreciated in him, his intelligence and wit and all that had been held in high esteem, were no longer respected nor sought after. He paid dearly for his actions in the solitude that lasted the rest of his life.

This experience was important for my growth, even at that young age, I knew it was up to me to carry myself as a victim or victor. I chose to learn from the molestation, never again agreeing to another's silent secrets. It served me well, years later, when an unknown person was stalking me. Every morning before work I would see the same man at the same time following me. He would dart in and out of traffic just to get behind me or to the side of me in traffic. He made it very obvious that he wanted his presence known to me.

I was not sure of his exact intentions; I only knew that he was very blatant in his attempts to intimidate me with fear. Instead of being afraid, I spoke with my dad, who told me to get his license plate number. After doing so, he called a police officer that he knew and had it traced. By the following day, the man had been contacted, warned and never showed up around me again.

Many times we put ourselves into a victim role, expecting the worse and getting it. We need to regain our connection with "God" and know that we are never victims of circumstance. But it's not something that ever goes away. Every time I think I've mastered the concept of creating my own reality, I'm given yet another opportunity to prove this lesson to myself.

Here is another example. This time, Michael gave me an experience that I would rather have learned differently and in a less painful way.

My dear friend Holly, a consultant in the candle business, invited me to join her at one of her bookings. We had conducted "candle/angel" parties before and it seemed to be a welcome addition to her business as well as a way for me to promote my business. It began with the usual pleasantries and introductions after which Holly gave her presentation.

Once Holly had concluded her portion of the evening, many of the ladies present began asking questions about my work and the connection that I have with angels, spirits, and so on. Things seemed to be going along as usual. I told them a little about myself and how I got started, as well as how their own intuitive abilities could be developed further. As I have said, doing this type of work requires my heart to be wide open so that I may accurately and precisely align with Michael and any spirits present who wish to communicate with me.

Suddenly, I felt an enormous amount of negative energy emanating from one of the guests in particular and knew immediately that she felt very negatively confronted by my presence. Working with people's skepticism is a pretty common part of my job until they can discern for themselves the authenticity behind my work. I thus engaged in a conversation with this woman, working with what I thought was an openness on her part toward my work. Despite her negativity, it seemed as though she was interested in what I was saying to the group of ladies. However, at the very same time, I was feeling a strong judgment from her against me.

I asked whether she disagreed with what I was saying, or if she had any questions that could clarify the open disdain she was feeling toward me. This is where it got a little hairy. It was my understanding that everyone at the party was open to me being there, sharing my work with them. This, I found out, was not exactly the case. This woman had known I was going to be there, and wanted to observe, but she was not open to my work or me. I am willing to have skeptics and cynics observe my methods, for I do not condemn or judge anyone's beliefs of faith; and, naively, I used to believe that this would be reciprocated.

I told this woman that if it was her wish for me to refrain from any interaction with her, I was willing to honor those feelings. At the same time, I requested that she also honor my presence, as well as the other guests who wished to interact with me, by abstaining from communication with me both verbally and mentally. She agreed, got up and went into the kitchen. However, when you're open to universal energy, it doesn't matter if you're physically near someone who is focusing his or her energy on you. The presence of energy is all around us, so naturally, this woman's conflict, which has been silently created, still hung in the air.

When she came back into the room, all seemed to be going well. Yet, I was continually brought back to her overwhelming energy. Finally, she explained her position and it was then that I found out she was devoutly religious. She explained to me that she did, indeed, believe from the accuracy of what she was hearing that I was undoubtedly communicating with angels and spirits. However, I was, "wrong for doing so."

I asked her why she had stayed around after the candle presentation if she felt I was wrong. Was she merely there to judge me? She said she was not judging me; she was interested in what I had to say. I explained that being interested when you have already condemned someone to being wrong is judgment.

I remained dejected by her confrontational energy; however, recognizing that I was in somebody else's home, I tried to be considerate of her beliefs while, at the same time, honoring my own. I had been doing workshops by this time, but always in my own home, in my own surroundings.

This confrontation left me feeling vulnerable and exposed, as though I was being fed to the lions.

The force of the energy emanating from this woman's condemnation and judgment overwhelmed me to such an extent that I instantly went to a place of hurt, fear, and vulnerability. Holly had assured me that I was welcome, but now I felt like a cruel joke had been played on me and that Michael had perpetrated it.

I felt how I imagine a stripper could feel when out of her element, as if I were doing a strip tease only to look down and find that I was not in a bar, but in a church. A stripper in a strip bar is completely appropriate. Stripping in a church? It's the complete opposite.

I shut down and closed myself off tightly. I felt like crying and running. Also, as I have mentioned, I felt betrayed by Michael. I pleaded with him, *Why didn't you tell me this was going to occur?*

Holly and I left in a hurry. She was frantically packing her candles while I was putting on a very strong face and saying my good-byes. Although I knew the others were interested in what I had to offer, I couldn't get to the car fast enough. After shutting the door, I burst into tears. I experienced every emotion possible: fear, vulnerability, and self-hatred for this part of me that was multi-dimensional. I also felt angry with Michael.

I felt like a complete victim of some sick trick to expose me and open me to great ridicule. My childhood tea experiences were running rampant in my mind. Upon later reflection, I understood what Michael was showing me. I still had a part of my wounded mind that said to me, "You are wrong if you do not exist in the eyes of religion."

I know that not to be true now, since religion is merely a highly restricted method of knowing "God" that is quite beneficial to many people. I simply do not fit into the category of needing a lot of external discipline. I have always been very self-disciplined. I felt victimized by this circumstance while going through it; however, I know how much that wound needed to be healed before I could and would further expose myself to larger groups of people who may hold very different views than my own. I now can look back with gratitude that Michael chose that environment to reveal my wound and not a larger arena, however painful it was that day.

13

Spiritual Guides — Who Are They?

I will begin this chapter with a story of how I began to really understand not only Archangel Michael but other spirit guides as well. "Once upon a time," I was deep into my spiritual quest, living a life of intuitive bliss with Jeff through the sharing of our heart connection. I had completed a spiritual course that helped me gain a deeper understanding of how to develop intuition through a method called kinesiology and was beginning to see the results in my life.

During these different courses, seminars, and studies I had been evaluating, I had also begun evaluating my life, where it was going, and where I wanted it to go. I knew I wanted to continue working; yet, I wanted more time with my two boys.

One summer, I got a message from Michael to call Jacob's school about setting him up for the new school year. I spoke with the Administrative Coordinator regarding his enrollment, and just as we were about to hang up, the counselor told me she was moving out of state and thought I would be a great candidate for her job. I wasn't interested, as I didn't want to work full time, but after some persuasion she convinced me of the benefits to working there, so I agreed to meet with her.

I didn't know it at the time, but this would become an instrumental building block in furthering my spiritual journey. I merely saw it as an opportunity to be with my children during the day and still make some money. "Coincidentally," the school also moved its location, so instead of driving my children through the heart of the town during rush-hour traffic, I would be driving only a half a mile from my house.

At the interview, I met the man I would be working for directly. I knew immediately that he was one of the main reasons I had been drawn to taking the job. I knew he was also the icing on the cake, and without a doubt, that was going to be a dear friend who would teach me many things I probably would not learn elsewhere. Our friendship grew from that point forward.

We had instant rapport as administrator and assistant, yet, our relationship became more of that of a spiritual mentor and collaborator. He was highly intelligent, as well as intuitive, and through him I was allowed to see how the mind and spirit can work in tandem. One afternoon at lunch, we were discussing work when, suddenly, the conversation turned to spirituality and spirit guides. I sensed two guides with us, one an Indian chief and the other an Asian woman, and I went into detail about their presence. He wasn't the least bit surprised and said he had known for many years that Yellow Eagle and Kuan Yin are with him. I was elated.

Here was a man whose opinion I very much respected, confirming I wasn't "out there." We spoke of our guides: who they are, where they come from, and what purpose they serve in our lives. This was only the beginning of many talks that helped each of us grow further in our spirituality, and I knew I needed to introduce this spiritual mentor of mine to the women in my spiritual "group" that had been meeting every other week for years.

Many years ago my mother, Lisa, and I went to California to attend a "woman's weekend" workshop with 200 other women from all over the country. In this weekend, we learned how to honor and cherish who we are, personally as women, how we interact with other women, and our perceived relationships with men. I had taken this course as one of my "last ditch" efforts to help save my first marriage with Kirk. Ultimately, that first marriage faltered. However, the course nevertheless, helped me to acknowledge that self-respect and honor of myself must always come first.

The three of us realized we needed to continue supporting one another, as well as other women, in the endeavors of our lives. We formed a group, together with the friend that had introduced us to this work, and had been meeting ever since. Over the years, some of the faces moved on and we would add some new ones, but the bonds that we built with these women remained stronger than ever.

At the time I issued my invitation to my boss and spiritual mentor, the growth of our group had become a bit stagnant. I knew that inviting my newfound friend into our group, with his wealth of knowledge, would alter and expand the dynamics of our spiritual group, as well as continue to encompass the support of our various relationships. The group welcomed him with open arms and what was once referred to as our "women's group" became a "group."

I did not facilitate this group. I had worked with everyone privately in sessions or through the workshops I led, but in our group my leadership had been set aside so we could share our intuitive abilities with one another as a whole. It was a safe place for us all to share our fears and victories. Undeniably, the foundation we built with one another has given us the courage and strength to get through many trials and tribulations while sharing the joys of everyday life.

Jeff aside, I first allowed my communication with Archangel Michael to be known in this group, and their ensuing confidence, patience, and support of my connection enabled me to hone my abilities, just as each of them were building communication with their own guides. The respect we had and still have for one another is mutual and highly regarded.

Learning the language of our guides is a lot like learning Spanish when all you know is English. It starts out slow and unclear: "foreign" in every sense of the word, until you understand the basics of the language and start building from there. At first, you're hearing Spanish and trying to translate it in your head to English and then speaking it back in Spanish. Much patience and fine-tuning are needed, but then, before long, you're not only speaking Spanish, you're bilingual.

Since every individual has their own guide and we're not all guided by the same one, I would like to share a few examples based upon my guide, my mom and sister's guides.

Archangel Michael: Overcoming Adversity

People guided by Michael can attest to the adversity that comes along in great proportions. Overcoming adversity through truth, honesty and integrity is our greatest challenge. We tend to become closed off, even appearing coldhearted at times, when we choose not to take Michael's challenge and push through it. We may go through a long period of time simply being stuck, somewhat like that of a defiant child, knowing what needs to be done but refusing to do it. I feel certain that, at these times of stagnation, Michael must be laughing at us, waiting patiently for us to align with his energy so we can once again push through whatever we've allowed to hold us back. The moment we do make a decision to align and be open for the truth, fortunately, we move forward very rapidly. Michael carries a high intensity of energy and if you allow it to come through, you will find he's masterful at manifesting what you desire, once you listen. I have been the example of this connection throughout the book.

Archangel Gabriel: Objectively sees both sides of any situation; great communicators

Gabriel has a unique way of providing all views. His primary field of expertise is aligning with those that have a difficult time knowing who they are in relationships. Most people guided by Gabriel are here to reveal both sides of any situation, to be mediators. An example could be that of a news reporter whose job it is to see all sides of the story while remaining objective. This is the challenge for those guided by Gabriel because, when they do take sides, they can appear very stubbornly "off the hook," logically finding reasons for not taking responsibility in the creation of their own reality. When in alignment, however, they are very loving, wonderful listeners who dispense sound advice.

Gabriel is also a trickster. Many times he will trick people into action when they have left neutral ground and chosen sides. Here is an example.

My mom, Sandy, is not only a wonderful asset for her listening abilities, but also for her ability to show us different ways of seeing things, as she did in her quest to quit smoking. Mom and I were in a session when my Grandma Bette, who passed away in 1974, came to me relaying the message that Mom was in danger of getting emphysema. Sandy's reaction to her mother's message was startling to me until I learned why. At a recent doctor's appointment, her doctor had given her the very same message. Prior to this, Gabriel had let her know it was time to stop smoking. Now this had been twice confirmed. With Gabriel's help, I guided her through the process of quitting.

After 38 years of smoking and various failed attempts throughout those years to quit, her temporary successes had lasted anywhere from a couple weeks to about four months before she would resume the habit once again. Needless to say, Mom preferred the quickest, easiest, and least challenging method available. The instructions given to us by Gabriel were very specific, not that easy, and extremely challenging.

Two weeks from the day of the session, on a Saturday, Mom was instructed to buy a carton of strong, unfiltered cigarettes and smoke one after another until the carton was gone. Immediately, she chose the path of logic and a multitude of reasons why she didn't really need to stop smoking presented themselves. Incredulous at what was being asked of her, she wondered if it was really worth it and whether there was anyone on this planet actually capable of physically fulfilling what Gabriel was instructing her to do! Putting logic aside, she asked Gabriel if this method was indeed her path and, after affirming its accuracy, followed through with his instructions, consequences and all.

True to form of anyone guided by Gabriel, and choosing not to stay neutral, Mom went in and out of stubborn logic. Throughout the week her mind would come up with horrific scenarios about what she could expect. During this time, she received a phone call from her aunt and uncle saying they would be in town for the weekend and that they would like to stay with her and my dad. Mom was elated.

The visit was a true gift from "God" since this particular aunt had always been a great spiritual inspiration and mentor to my mother, someone who, as it happens, was also guided by Gabriel. The two of them made plans to be together on the day Mom was to begin the process of quitting smoking "The Gabriel way." Knowing she wouldn't have to go through this experience alone was enough for Mom to change her perception and actually see the possibility of success.

On that fateful Saturday, I received a phone call. Mom was riddled with angst. Plans had fallen through and it was no longer just she and her aunt. It appeared that every time the path was cleared, circumstances placed yet another seemingly unavoidable obstacle in front of her that kept throwing her back into logic. The task at hand looked too huge and painful to undergo. We discussed where her anxieties were coming from and how, at times, Gabriel has a warped sense of humor when showing the opposing view, especially when his messages are received with an unwillingness to stay neutral.

I encouraged Mom to focus on her desire to give up cigarettes and reassured her of "God" and Gabriel's presence throughout the process. Amazingly enough, the message changed and Gabriel, the trickster, had now determined she only had to smoke three packs of cigarettes in quick succession. This did little to ease her mind. Three packs or a carton; what was the difference? The two options both screamed, "Impossible!" Mom did, however, accept her message, found neutral ground, and started smoking "the Gabriel way." Three cigarettes into her first pack, she was in her backyard puking her guts out and wondering how she was going to lift another cigarette to her lips, let alone smoke it! The message came through, loud and clear, that her task was complete.

The enormity of Gabriel's message and Mom's perception of it sent her into such calamity that she wasn't able to see the simplicity of the plan. The trickster had come to call again. Mom's test was whether she could stay objective to the message she had been given, or if she was going to choose sides and live in the chaos of her own mind.

When Mom finally chose to accept the message without any judgments, she didn't have to continue. She also learned that she was strong enough in her connection to physically go through this alone, without anybody holding her hand and telling her that everything would be okay. The trust she had placed in herself and Gabrielle resulted in the accomplishment of her heart's desire to be a non-smoker. I am pleased to announce that she has been smoke-free ever since and remains a healthy, living, true inspiration to us all!

Mother Mary: Powerful nurturers

Mother Mary is there to nurture, support, and motivate in a very powerful way and using whatever means possible to accomplish that goal. The most important aspect of Mary to understand, however, is that without self-nurturing, there is nothing to give. Those guided by Mother Mary will often become insecure and second-guess every move they make if they do not first nurture themselves.

Lisa (my sister), is a woman you want on your side. She allows people in her life to move to great heights while nurturing them along the way. Her nurturing, however, does not always look like the conventional view of nurturing. When Lisa gets a message, beware! You will know it. Many times he "nudging" of us to become all that we can be, feels confronting and abrasive, it seems to be anything but a nurturing nudge. Like it or not, you can count on her to make sure you do not stay stagnant for long. Lisa simply "tells it like it is" and does exactly what is needed without second-guessing herself. At times, Lisa is not even aware that she is receiving a message from Mother Mary. However, when she is in a place where her own self-nurturing has been put on the back burner, she will begin to practice self-destructive behavior. In these instances, she second-guesses herself without knowing or acknowledging that she is doing it. She must remain conscious of what will nurture her in any given situation in order to keep herself in alignment.

14

Following Guidance

My understanding is that "God" gave us these guides to help us in our spiritual journey just as he also gave us our parents for our human journey. I want to be clear that when I refer to the angels who assist me in my spiritual journey, they are to be honored for their assistance and not meant to be worshiped.

Either an angel or an ascended master guides all of us, but "God" gives us our personal guide for a specific reason. We all have a mission to accomplish while we are here on Earth. The guide who we have been given is "assigned," for lack of a better term, to each of us for that mission or set of life lessons to which we desired in our plan with "God" before our arrival on the Earth plane. Putting it into very simple terms, if our main mission in this life is to overcome strong adversities, you would be given Archangel Michael as your guide. He has many guides under him that are assisting you, also, though you may not know each of them on a one-on-one basis.

It is much like going to a specific college based upon what you desire to do for your profession. For example, if you wanted to be a dentist, you would choose a specific school that would benefit your career choice. "God" has made sure that who guides us by is directly related to our life purpose or mission. I have been given some specific characteristics of the guides with whom I have worked. These characteristics have been compiled from those messages as well as the work I have done with my clients over the years.

There are times when I am very confronted by the fact that "God" gave me Michael. Each guide has predominant characteristics that are associated solely with each. Michael represents truth, honesty, integrity, the love for challenges, and overcoming of adversity. It takes a lot of trust for me to listen to the guidance of Archangel Michael.

One of my first major challenges after discovering my connection with Michael was the "blessing/challenge" of my second husband Jeff. As I said, before marriage, he was very encouraging of me and my quest for this newfound "knowledge," but after I began to align with Michael, he started getting nervous about my revelation. To him, it was like I had just fallen off a spaceship and was telling him I was communicating with aliens regularly.

The truth is that he probably would have accepted a story of space aliens, since he leaned more toward science fiction than spirituality. Angels were more than a little confrontational for his disposition. At first, it was not a big deal because we were still sharing our hearts. However, that was all to change.

Jeff was never abusive however when I placed a judgment on myself as "different," I unfortunately felt it from everywhere and especially from him. Our connection started to deteriorate, and without my husband to share my experiences as I had had before, I started feeling scared and unsure of myself.

"God" gave us free will to make our own decisions, and when I met Jeff, I had definitely made a choice to not look strange or different to anyone. But things change, and we must adapt to those changes. At this point, I was 31 years old, on my second marriage, and I realized I couldn't deny my connection to "God" any longer. Looking back, I was epically scared of this part of me. When I finally not only knew, but understood that it was my destiny to expand my communication with Michael out from privacy and into the outside world that included my family, friends, and future clients, I became deathly afraid, just as that little girl had, years before, during her tea parties.

At this time, my experience of "God," in terms of religion, was limited. My mother had converted to Catholicism for my father's sake, and they had been married in a Catholic church, so we went to church on most Sundays. My mother went to the church for the main Mass and Lisa and I went to catechism. My father only attended church with us on Easter, Christmas, and various other holidays. I had received my First Communion, even though I had no idea who "God" was.

My sister seemed to have a real grasp of "God." Lisa looked forward to going to church, attending classes, and receiving her First Communion and Confirmation. My mother wanted Lisa to attend and conform to the foundation Catholicism offered. I perceived that my mother thought it was less important that I establish the same foundation. In the wake of this, the part of me that felt unwanted at birth and not "good enough" resurfaced again.

Several years later I asked my mom why she didn't encourage me to go to church as she had with Lisa. Her response was that she honestly did not know. Upon further reflection, she supposed it was because she could see where the discipline of the church would benefit Lisa, but didn't feel that it was necessary for me to pursue the same path. It was later revealed to me, through Michael, that "God" and he work through my "knowing," so the more I know intellectually, from studying and lessons learned in organized religions, the more I second guess the "knowing" of my heart. This diagnosis has been proven true time and time again.

Jeff was my first challenge to my path of relying on and following the truth within me. Unfortunately, the challenge was a lot for me to handle, so my logic prevailed and I thought the only path at that time was to separate from him so I could pursue my heart's dream of experiencing the "God" within me.

Jeff and I sold our house, he moved in with friends, and the boys and I moved in with my parents. Thank "God" that Adam and Jacob were sure of my connection with "God" and Michael, by this time, or things would have been a lot worse. Many times before, they had received proof that my connection with Archangel Michael and "God" was authentic. However, one particular incident before my separation from Jeff confirmed it for them.

Jeff had already gone to work when the boys and I woke up one morning to find our dog Sammy paralyzed on the floor of her sleeping room with her eyes puffed out. Her legs were stiff as boards and she was in great pain. She would whimper at any touch. We had no idea what was wrong with her. We thought perhaps a spider had bitten her.

I asked Michael, *What do I do?* He peacefully walked me through a step-by-step procedure. He directed me as to where to place my hands, which became very warm (almost hot) in order to draw the energy out of her legs, and then instructed me to place my hands over her eyes. The process took approximately 15 minutes, but it seemed like a lifetime. When Michael said to stop, Sammy quickly jumped up and walked away as if nothing had happened.

Sammy never had a problem again. Jacob, Adam, and I were simply astounded at the miracle we had just experienced. I don't know what had made Sammy ill. What I do know is that it was a test for me to follow through with my faith in Michael and "God." This was just one of many instances we had experienced up to this point. My sons knew what I knew, so there was nothing to debate. Jeff, however, when told of this experience, was still not buying the whole angel story.

At any rate, Jeff and I remained in contact during our separation. Neither of us was willing to start divorce proceedings. We still didn't agree on our paths, so we were butting heads about what to do. Every time I asked Michael whether or not it was time to divorce Jeff, the answer was always "no."

It was five months into our separation before I could see the truth about how my judging myself and being right about my path was causing Jeff to question our marriage. It became quite clear to me the night he said to me, "I didn't marry Michael; I married you." I astutely learned a huge lesson about not judging someone else's path to "God" when it doesn't match your own, and conversely, no one has the right to judge your path either. I now know whatever Jeff's experience with "God" is, it is his, not mine, just as mine is not his. As fulfilling as it was for me to re-embrace this lost part of myself, he didn't understand it, because he doesn't experience Angels or Spirits. The truth is that many people don't, and they may never let themselves.

Jeff is extremely artistic and uses his intuition when it comes to machinery and fabricating cars. His path is incredible in its own right, yet I am not drawn to his intuitive path. We all have an intuitive side to our brain, but we may not use it in the same way. From that day forward, I could see his side of things. My mistake, if there even is such a thing, was judging my own path of spirituality as wrong because it didn't match his which opened me up to feel emotional criticism. He, in turn, became extremely defensive about his own experience and directed his judgment toward me.

The learning experience we all gained from these five months of separation was tremendous. Most important, we learned that we had love for one another and hoped that would be enough. We agreed to disagree about our path of intuitive awakening. After five long months of constant reflection, we also agreed that we both wanted to attempt to make our marriage work.

15

Spirit, Mind, Body Connection

Michael has guided me to four attributes of a person that helps us to achieve the Spirit, Mind, Body Connection. The first begins with a purely loving, peaceful state in which you feel comfort, divine love and safety. I find this state by communicating with Michael. Though, many people find it in a place or a circumstance that will assist them in getting there, such as a garden or possibly a safe relationship.

Once this loving state of existence is established, the second attribute that is evident is clarity of messages. In this state, undeniable, clear messages are received as to what you need to do, accomplish, or simply know for progress. Personally, I first receive messages through my knowing. Then, a visual picture will be presented if I have any doubt in my knowing. Others receive their messages differently.

The third attribute is an absence of fear. This is where most people falter. The fearless mode of consciousness consists of letting go of any and all attachments to the message given. When you do not necessarily want or like the message you have been given, it is likely that you will get stuck in this phase. With fear, this anxious state can last for a minute, a day, or even years.

I am well aware of this state since, throughout the years, I have been digging my feet in, so to speak, when I do not like a message or method that I know will further my growth. I knew, many years ago, when Jeff and I separated, that I couldn't deny Michael's existence in our marriage for long. However, the fear of being divorced again and letting go of him did not sit well with me.

I stopped my growth in this area of my life, deciding to deal with it later, hoping and waiting for either him to change or hoping that, somehow, it would not matter. Neither occurred. We must remember that when we receive a divine message, the message does not change, no matter how much we want it to or try to stop it. It is a message from "God," not from our mind. The fourth and final attribute is living passionately with the message or vision you have received. This passion must come from a conviction that is unwavering. Along with a fearless disposition, not living passionately is also where people can easily get stuck. At this point, people will often begin questioning their message. This may be the hardest attribute of successful living to master because you must be so passionately drawn to your message that no one can pull you from believing it to be true.

This phase is where I have wavered many times. I wavered at many different times because in those times, I did not have many people in my life, my second husband included, who had experienced angels as I had. Because of a lack of support, I began limiting my experiences with Michael and the other angels so that it would be less confronting to my husband and others. From almost the beginning of my marriage to Jeff, I received a message that it was time to embrace my gift of intuition and Archangel Michael.

People I both know and don't know have asked me many times, "Why can't you just refer to Michael as 'Spirit or intuition'?" This has been asked of me in order to protect me, so that I do not "look weird" to others, and at times, I have agreed, so I have tried it as they suggested. The price, however, has been my authenticity with myself. I no longer will waste my time and energy appeasing others' discomfort at the risk of my own integrity. In order to shift to Spirit, Mind, Body, you must listen to your heart's desire instead of your mind's belief system. Your heart will never betray you, always giving you an authentic desire to move through a situation of judgment that perhaps the mind has stored as your belief; it is unwilling to be challenged. In order to spiritually progress, it becomes imperative to challenge your mind's belief system. What holds us back, almost always, is either someone else's truth or an old wound that is stubbornly trying to hold on to the prison of the mind. This does not allow true freedom. All Mind, Body, Spirit connections will, at some point in your life, need to be transformed into Spirit, Mind, Body. This is the only authentic connection that will not give you pain and suffering. Pure wisdom is the way of Spirit, Mind, Body connection.

The hierarchy makes sense. The heart uses the mind that, in turn, uses the body to manifest the heart's desire.

This process begins with the concept that the heart is the place in which our true connection with "God" begins. The mind is the tool "God" has given us to discern the desires our heart wishes to manifest. The logical mind, in its truest form without judgment will discern the best path to take in order to fully manifest our heart's desire without effort or strain.

The logical mind that has judgment is the so- called "negative side" of us, or darkness. When we choose the path of darkness, we are establishing a right or wrong orientation to events in our life. Getting stuck here will create emotional wounds and pain from which we learn to clearly discern the path we want to take. Some individuals simply choose the path of least resistance by communicating with their heart, "God," Angelic Realm, etc.

With great trust, these people can move forward and their heart's desire very quickly and easily. "God" has no attachment to which path we take. We have free will, which occurs in the logical mind, enabling us to learn through either lightness or darkness.

Our logical mind, when it comes into contact with something it determines to be opposing to our belief system, must do only what it knows to do: choose judgment (separation) or discernment (facts). If an emotional wound shows up that the logical mind can accept and work on, it will surface so it can be understood and healed. In order to do so, it must return to past experiences so that the emotion can be cleared, allowing the heart to fulfill and manifest its desires.

If, however, this opposing force is denied access by an open and healing mind, and thus determined to be "wrong," the mind will judge itself as though it is judging others. The only reason we believe the logical mind and make judgments is because of a disconnection from the heart or from "God," which are one and the same. The heart never feels pain or judges something as right or wrong. The mind is what tells you to feel the emotions of pain or pleasure. Everything is relative. If there is no past experience or teaching with which to relate, the mind will choose the proper path of discernment, manifesting the heart's desire as it was designed to do.

At the core of our existence, we are all diamonds. When our soul finds mud that has been slung on top of our bright and beautiful diamond, the natural reaction is to cleanse it. This is done in many ways. The most common way is to create a safe environment in which to speak your truth where judgment is not present. Unfortunately, many of us do not feel that there is a place in which this can be safely accomplished.

Therefore, we may engage in self-destructive behaviors such as drinking, smoking, overeating and many other forms of mudslinging, choosing to live in the mind or beneath the mud, believing this will stop the pain our soul is attempting to purge and heal. When one begins the sad process of self-destructive behavior, what inevitably occurs is more trouble, and more suffering, luckily and inevitably, the strong desire to remove the inauthentic parts of us that are keeping our diamond from shining brightly will return. Fortunately and unfortunately, however, this awakening sometimes only occurs after great pain and suffering. However, this process is entirely unnecessary.

I once had a client who was living in Mind, Body, Spirit. However, through the course of our working together, she transformed herself to Spirit, Mind, Body. Later, at a time when I needed financial assistance to further my business, I was given the message that she was the one to assist me. However, this appeared to me as a conflict of interest. Nevertheless, I removed my fear and doubt, and when I approached her with my need, she did not hesitate.

In the past, she would have questioned and worried about giving anyone a large sum of money since her experiences in this area had never benefited her. Her mind *still* felt the pain of these experiences. To both of our amazement, there was no doubt in either of our hearts that she was the one to assist me since (much to my amazement) she had also clearly received the same message to do so. Things worked out mutually beneficially, so I have asked her to share a bit of her journey and how she now experiences life.

In her words:

"I feel very blessed to have the opportunity to share my transformation from Mind, Body, Spirit to Spirit, Mind, Body. This was very difficult as I was a person who was very analytical and analyzed every aspect of my life. I was living my life from my shoulders up, or more truthfully, between my ears. My mind controlled my life. It told me how to feel, when to hurt, and what to do. My life was full of fear, shame, self-doubt, guilt, judgment and self-denial.

It convinced me of things that weren't true and that I was a victim to everything that happened in my life. The idea that I was undeserving and should withhold my love from myself was self-taught with the help of my mind.

I was constantly punishing myself for past mistakes. I was my own worst enemy. I wanted to be perfect because, for my entire life, I had been taught that only the people that are perfect are rewarded and will go to heaven. This belief system was well imprinted on me. I had internalized all I was taught and therefore didn't challenge any of it until recently.

I was raised a Methodist and never thought to explore other denominations. I changed churches from time to time, but never strayed from the faith. I would convince myself that a particular church was working for me even though I couldn't think about one thing that I liked about it. It wasn't bringing me fulfillment, and I wasn't taking away any messages that applied to my life.

After months of forced participation and not finding enjoyment, I found Lynn. She didn't disparage the church or its beliefs. She helped me open up to the possibilities of expanding on what I'd already been taught and discerning which beliefs were the truth for me and which were not. Lynn's messages hit home and helped me to enhance my spirit.

Prior to my work with Lynn, I had inherited my belief systems and never questioned whether I embraced their messages that, I now realize, had hindered my spiritual growth. My mind told me I couldn't question these beliefs and I didn't. I continued following these patterns, not because they were working, but because they were familiar and comfortable. Testing new waters took me out of my comfort zone. It was only when I was finally ready to move through the hurt and pain of my past, to design my life and fulfill my heart's desire, that I began the transformation.

I always needed to control every aspect of my life, determining the how and when of everything that happened. I was so sure I could do a better job than "God" could, that I shut Him out and dove deeper into my mind. I quit hearing the messages that He was trying to provide. I believed "God" was the core of my life because I was a Christian and I went to church on a regular basis. But, He was only in a physical building. I did not experience Him in my heart.

I was so afraid to trust myself and surrender to "God" that I gave my power to my mind and denied "God" within me. Transformation for me is like an artichoke. There are layers and layers that you cannot see. Just when you think you have peeled away your hidden agendas, issues, and fears, there are more layers to be shed. Fortunately, I had Lynn to help me shed those layers of hurt that had created a false sense of protection, and I was able to get to my heart.

I was eager to be in spirit and live my life in my heart and not my mind. In order to make this shift, I had to listen to the desires of my heart as opposed to my mind's beliefs. I begged "God" to help me and learned how not to deny my connection with Him and to love myself through the process. I accepted that there are lessons, both positive and negative, to be learned. Wisdom is gained through failure, and it is also through wisdom that we learn to handle our successes. Surrendering my mind to "God" allows me to know my truth.

It took me a long time to see the spirit in me that I allowed others to see. I loved my friends, family, and strangers unconditionally, but I had a different set of rules for myself. I was to be perfect and it was unacceptable to have failures. I believed everything was my fault and I gave up my very being to be accepted by others. Then, once I gave up my self-respect and spirit for another, they didn't like who I became.

The light went on. Living this human experience is about being who I am and respecting myself and not denying "God" in me for anyone. I am a gift from "God," a gift to be honored. I have to first honor my desires and truths before people will honor me just as I am. I no longer have to be perfect in order to speak my truth. "God" is always with me, even if others do not agree with or like who I am.

What does this transformation mean to me? When anything happens or I receive messages, I ask for "God's" guidance, meaning that I start with Spirit. If it is through Spirit that the message comes, I am at peace and follow through with the desires of "God" for I know that we are one and these are my true desires. If I begin to get cloudy and start analyzing, I know that the message comes from my mind, and I once again surrender to "God."

Is life perfect now that I have experienced this transformation? It is not as my mind had previously defined perfection. I am at peace with my life and am grateful for the comfort of "God" in it. Loving myself unconditionally will give me freedom, both spiritually and personally, and this is what I intend for myself.

I am now attending a church of a different faith, not because the faith of my childhood is wrong, but because this is where I hear my truth. I heard the following and found it very powerful: "Love should be a free gift from "God" and others."

I thank "God" for my gifts. I am a planner, but I now know that "God" is a much better planner than I am and I trust my life to Him."

Patti

16

Creating Your Dreams

It is imperative to understand that we create our own reality, be it a pleasant or not-so-pleasant experience. "God" gives us the ability to create the circumstances that our higher consciousness feels is needed for our highest level of growth. So, often we find ourselves in situations or circumstances that we believe are beyond our control, convincing ourselves that we aren't responsible for being in the midst of what we don't want.

People who continue to believe that someone or something outside of themselves is creating their environment are, in essence, saying that they are victims of something greater than "God." There is nothing greater than "God." Once we truly know and embrace the fact that we are co-creators with this force, we can see the inaccuracies in our previous beliefs. I have come to recognize that knowing this concept is not enough for me, so Michael makes sure I experience that which I teach.

Manifesting my desires has never been too challenging. However, recognizing I deserve what I manifest is another story.

A month into my second marriage, Jeff and I purchased a house. Prior to this, we had spoken with a real estate agent describing what we wanted and the price we were able to pay. What we were shown in our price range came nowhere near to what I knew my home was to look like. I knew not to settle and that the home I saw us living in was just on the horizon. Mind you, at this time my concept of Archangel Michael as my guide was purely what I called a "gut instinct." Also, the concept of humans being co-creators with "God" ran more along the lines of "pure luck" bordering on "maybe there's something more to this than just pure luck."

After seeing yet another house and feeling the seeds of doubts starting to creep in, I drove by an intersection with a canopy on the corner and a real estate agent showing HUD home listings. I pulled in, and much to my delight, I spoke with a woman who was as committed to my dream home as I. She had no limitations, just possibilities. Days later she called with some listings for me to look over and when we pulled up to the third house, I knew we'd found it.

At this time, Jeff and I had not yet been pre- qualified. We were told that, if we could get qualified and approved within two weeks, we could get $900 of our money back, and if within three weeks, we could get $600 back. The Realtor was shooting for three weeks. I was shooting for two.

We had our loan and were moved in within two weeks, much to the awe of just about everyone, including Jeff, who, if truth be told, didn't want to buy a house in the first place because of his financial fears. Another masterful link provided by Michael? Absolutely. Did I know it was Michael at the time? No.

Jeff always had a difficult time believing that you can create whatever you want. Furthermore, he believed that if, by some stroke of genius, a person did create it, it would be a struggle to keep it. I, on the other hand, held the belief that such maneuvers do not have to be a struggle. Interestingly enough, however, I did have a core belief that I didn't deserve success without a struggle. In a perfect Universe, this would have been an ideal time to realize that my successful co-creations were made with "God," and not Jeff.

We lived in this house for quite a few years but needless to say our old beliefs crept in and we found ourselves at opposite ends of the spectrum trying to hold on to our different beliefs until finally succumbing and buying into our logic. It was, at that time that our marriage was also breaking down. My heart's desire for the life that I knew awaited me and Jeff's reality of life didn't support each other. We decided to sell our home in order to reconcile our financial differences and doubts, and we moved our family into a two-bedroom apartment. Our life together seemed to be on the mend with the financial stressors gone or were we just pacifying ourselves. Neither of us really wanted to move into the confines of apartment life after having a roomy house with a big backyard and a pool. However, we were cleaning up our financial woes and thus thought we would have to bide our time before buying another house.

The fact that my sister and her children lived in a house about a half a mile away made the transition a lot smoother.

This allowed my boys to ride their bikes or roller blades to her house at any time.

In the meantime, Jeff encouraged me to do my intuitive consulting out of our apartment. He even came up with ideas that would help me to build my business. I was elated to finally have his support to pursue my dream career and things were looking up.

We lived in that apartment for approximately nine months when the decision to renew the lease arose. It was about this time that Lisa and her family were moving into a new rental house up north and we were helping her move. I walked into the house she was moving into, and thought how I wished another rental like this one would become available in the neighborhood.

Two months later, when we absolutely had to make a decision regarding another lease, the house next door to Lisa's, one that was nearly identical to hers, came up for rent. I was ecstatic. I loved the house she was living in, and to be right next door would be a dream come true. Well, at least it would be for Lisa and me. Our husbands, on the other hand, were less than thrilled. Yet, being the good sports that they were and seeing that we spent almost every day together anyway, they consented.

Creativity doesn't stop when you achieve your goal. As with breathing, you don't stop just because you've taken one breath. You continue with the next, and the next and the next. I was given the opportunity to observe my alignment with "God" and how far I'd progressed in staying centered in my creativity.

My point in describing the details of this and other experiences is to show how often people stay in their logic, fretting over, seemingly important yet ultimately inconsequential things that very often only appear to be valid, yet ultimately have unsettling consequences for our peace of mind.

When our lease was up a couple years later the next message I received of purchasing a new home was a bit more challenging. Michael initially gave me the date of June 17th, as the date I would be moving into my new home. Again, this date seemed impossible for many of the logical reasons, with finances being at the top of the list. Jeff at that time was adamant about not buying a house and in truth probably never would have wanted to again since he hadn't dealt with his old wounds from the last experience. I on the other hand, am always processing and working to heal my issues. I knew by this point in my life to follow Michael's messages, yet I still questioned my sanity at doing so in the face of Jeff's less-than-optimistic outlook.

Michael continued to move me forward in what needed to be done to start the process. Meanwhile, I dealt with the reactions of the many people who were truly concerned as to how we were going to do this. I felt insecure and sometimes downright ridiculous when telling them that I was being guided and that now was the time to buy. However, Michael continued to provide everything for me as long as I followed his guidance, which at many times I did not want to do. At that point, we went about getting pre-qualified for a house.

Amazingly, this was not as difficult as I had anticipated, so the search for our new home continued.

I contacted, a friend and realtor, and looked at house after house. Yet, every time she found one that fit the needs of our family and my business needs, invariably, the asking price would be too much or they would have already accepted another bid. After about a week of continuous mind chatter, such as, *What house is the right house, how am I going to do this? or Jeff is being confronted,* and so on, I finally snapped out of it and remembered that "God" was in charge of this process and that all I had to do was surrender, and all would be provided for.

Everything then fell back into place and we found the most beautiful home that far exceeded what I believed was possible. However, many more complications occurred that led me to believe we were not going to get the house by the seventeenth, as I had been told.

Despite these occurrences, Michael kept reassuring me that this was an accurate message and to hold tight to the truth. Whenever I doubted Michael, my wonderful sister Lisa would ask, over and over again, "What is the date?" making me repeat it to her so as not to lose sight of the truth.

At this time, the lender had assured us that a contract could be written up so that we would not have to come up with a down payment. Then, one day, that became "not true." Three weeks before closing, the lender told us that we did need a down payment, and how much money down would be needed, and frankly, we didn't have it. I got a new message: through my father I was to approach my uncle with the possibility of loaning us the money. I thought, *Why do I have to do this?*

I don't like asking for help, and though I loved my uncle, he wasn't known for his generosity with money. After I wore myself out with the internal battle taking place inside my head, I finally surrendered. What did I really have to lose? The worst my uncle could do was say, "no" and I would then just wait for Michael's next message.

The degree, to which my heart opened up, when my uncle readily agreed, was indescribable. I realized then, what a gift this loan would be for each of us: for me, it was a gift to be able to ask for help, and for my uncle, it was a gift to be able to give. Well, after this blessing, one would think it would be smooth sailing from there, right? Wrong.

The original lender, who had assured us that all was going well, called up two and a half weeks prior to my June 17th date. The lender said that it was now impossible to go ahead with the loan; there was some bureaucratic red tape with the financing. I remember thinking, *Is this ever going to end?*

Then, "God" provided Jeff and I with a friend whose husband knew a different lender we could try. Miracles do happen when you step beyond judgment. We were introduced to a man who wouldn't take "no" for an answer. His spirit knew no bounds. Our new lender jumped through hoops in tying up the loose ends, never faltering in his mission to get us our home. It wasn't until the last day of closing that he began to have his doubts. We had only two hours to record the documents before the office closed for the weekend. The seventeenth was the next day and we had already given notice to our rental home with no place to go.

My lender told me that he didn't think we were going to be able to get it through until Monday or Tuesday. I asked Michael what to do. His reply was to leave the office, go home and finish packing. He assured me that it was going to be done and I would be moving the next day. Michael's message was completely accurate. My lender called me an hour and a half later and said, "Congratulations, it's recorded." His other comment was, "Wow, when you know something, you know it!"

Both the lender and I were forever changed from that experience. I have since referred several clients of mine to him. He has told them that there is nothing that can stop him after our experience together. Let me reassure you that he has proven that true. In retrospect, I can see that all the doubts, mind chatter, and the questioning of my sanity had to occur for me to really grasp how much Michael is with me and to also see how the Universe works with other humans in this endeavor. I now proceed with my life confidently remembering that chaos doesn't always have to represent frenzy in my life. It is possible to find peace within the chaos.

My son Jacob had wanted a Basset hound for as long as I could remember. We had had dogs before this time, and the experiences had been both pleasant and not so pleasant. Jeff wasn't at all pro-dog. Whereas I, on the other hand, didn't have a problem with getting a new dog as long as it was Jacob's dog and not mine.

So, Jacob set out "creating" his dog. We discussed how if it was in the highest interest for all, he and "God" would manifest his desires. But, under no circumstances, were we to be his source of "reality making." If he was going to manifest this dog, it wasn't going to be through our buying it for him. He had done previous research on how much a basset hound could cost and found it could be upwards of $1,300.

Jacob didn't give up. Jeff and I still weren't in agreement about pets and whether Jacob was responsible enough to take care of one. But, then again, Jeff didn't believe in manifesting through one's heart's desire to begin with. So he didn't see harm in Jacob's trying to do so. I, on the other hand, knew that we would indeed be getting a dog and got the message, "Summer." As it was only September at that time, I wasn't too worried about Jacob manifesting his dream; summer seemed far enough away to let me relax.

It was then, in October, that we got a call from my mother saying that a woman at work had three Basset hound puppies that she had found. She was looking to find them homes, at no cost. Coincidence? I believe not. What were we going to do? Jeff and I talked it over. Though he wasn't at all for it, he agreed, but only after setting boundaries as to where the dog could and could not be in the house. We didn't tell Jacob, as we wanted it to be a surprise. We were going to pick the dog up on a Friday night and have it here waiting for him when he got home. That Thursday, out of the blue, Jacob informed us that he was getting a dog the next day. There was no way he could possibly know how impressed I was with his connection to his guide, but on the other hand, I was questioning my own, since I had clearly gotten the message "summer."

We brought the dog home and when Jacob walked into his room, our family plus my niece and nephew sang, "Happy Dog Day To You" to the tune of "Happy Birthday." Jacob was elated, wearing a smile brighter than any I had seen in a long while. I asked him what he was going to name her, and he told us that there was a girl named "Summer" on Baywatch that he really liked. That's how his dog, "Summer," came to be. Obviously, my message was accurate. It was my interpretation of the message that was off.

Life should have been bliss, but something was missing. Jeff and I seemed to be once again drifting apart in spite of all that we had achieved. We had become mechanical in our interactions and we both knew it. After so much work on attempting to bridge the gap of our spiritual differences I got the message that we would be divorcing. Our time together had run its course. My judgments came rushing at me with full force. How could Michael do this to me? Why hadn't he told me when we married in the first place that it would only last seven years? I told Michael if I had known it wasn't going to be for a lifetime then I wouldn't have married Jeff in the first place. I value marriage so very much and didn't want to be divorced once, much less twice.

Obviously, by conducting private intuitive sessions out of my home, people were bound to discover that Jeff and I were no longer living together. It's not that I was ashamed of the choice he and I had made; we were both certain that it was the path we needed to take. What was plaguing me was the judgment that I was placing upon myself for being a so-called "spiritual" consultant who was going through a second divorce. How would that look to people? More important, how did it look to me?

17

The Final Step

The message that my marriage was at an end came as a huge surprise to me. At that time, I was completely unaware of how judgmental I was being about the state that my marriage had deteriorated into, and I had therefore chosen to ignore the final signs. I had been doing this work for many years at that time, building it from scratch through word of mouth. But even though it had become successful in its own right, the lingering strains of my financial situation were clearly showing me that there was still something holding me back from embracing all of myself and my truth.

Jeff had been supportive of me in the way he knew how, but was continuously confronted by the work that I was doing. As much as he loved "the person" Lynn, he still could not come to grips with the fact that I communicated with Archangel Michael and had such faith in his messages that I willingly followed them without question.

To Jeff's credit, he had been extremely patient with the process it took for me to build my clientele. Though we were both working very hard, his negative feelings regarding my work were making it difficult for me to prosper; I took no confidence in knowing that all he wanted was for me to make money.

It's ironic that when Jeff and I first began dating, money didn't hold the power he started to give it as our life continued together. When we first dated, he was driving what he called his "Galactic Cruiser" (a beat up old Buick) and was happy doing so. I can now see that in my desires for a nice home and vehicles, I had played a part in his consciousness shifting from being financially laid back to being more money driven; his standard of living had been raised during our marriage, and this created financial pressure he had never experienced.

I do my work because I love doing it. Money is a byproduct of that love, and any and all financial success manifests from that love. Jeff's experience of work lies in his interest to pay bills and get ahead so that he can enjoy life with fewer struggles. I now can understand his point. However, it was a catch 22 for me at that time: I wanted to pay our bills as much as he did, but it was that our methods doing so that differed and we couldn't agree to disagree and come up with a resolution that would be a compromise for both our standards.

My experience of putting my heart first and allowing the abundance to flow was too "out of touch with reality" for his logical approach. It was simply not working for us. I was falling into my logical mind every time I dealt with Jeff regarding my work and what I felt guided to do.

If I make my work about money, I lose the intent my heart has for helping those in need, whether or not they have the financial means to pay my fees. If I were to focus on the ends, it would make what I do a job, instead of the dream of my heart. I knew, through Michael, that I would do very well financially only if I did my work from a position of love and unity with "God," but the financial success was never and never will be my first intention. I was not able to communicate this to Jeff, especially with his lack of support, which over time started coming through in belittling comments or even more so in the sarcastic tone in which he said them. He would say, "Why don't we ask Archangel Michael what we should do?" or "Maybe Michael will give you some money."

One day, in particular, I was feeling the pull, more than usual, to make money. I felt I was being made to go against my own heart. It felt shameful to fall into Jeff's logical reasons for why I should promote my business. After all, Michael had always led me to the path that would be in my best interest. He had even led me in how to promote myself, which I knew to be through word of mouth, and also in writing this book. Doing it the way Jeff wanted me to felt horrible.

On one particular morning, a very dear friend of mine was visiting from out of town. Jeff and I were still married at this time; we hadn't yet made the final decision to separate. My friend and I were discussing my financial situation and all its bleakness. We were working on finding the deep issue underneath my block, when her husband, who has become a dear friend over the years, called.

He said something that didn't make any sense to me at all. He asked me if I had an old boyfriend named Anthony. I searched my memory and it came up empty. I said, "No." He said he needed to relay an intuitive message he'd received. He said there was something incomplete between an old boyfriend named Anthony and me. Not wanting to hinder my friend's helpful intuitive message, I replied, "Huh, I don't know; maybe it's an old boyfriend's middle name or something!" We dropped the subject and moved on to discuss other issues.

Later, as we were going to dinner, we were driving past the house of an old boyfriend who I had dated 19 years ago. I mentioned to my friend that while we were dating, he and his best friend had been in a car accident and his best friend had died. I wondered how he was doing now since his friend's death had really taken a toll on him and we had broken up shortly afterward.

Five days later, while attending a lecture during "Spirit Week" at a church, I was mesmerized by the guest minister who was speaking and his fiancée who was an incredible singer. The connection these two people shared was palpable. You could feel Spirit connecting their hearts as they shared themselves with the audience. The deep emotion I felt was beyond explanation and I remember thinking to myself, "I'm going to have that."

I had been waiting at least three years now for Jeff and I to regain the heartfelt connection we had had during our first years of marriage. I was living in my connection to Michael and "God," believing that was enough to sustain my heart.

Unfortunately, I had been logically approaching my marriage with Jeff, just as he was living in his logical mind and shutting his heart off to me completely. I didn't realize until that very moment, sitting in the audience watching these two beautiful souls share their hearts so openly, how much I had been living in my logical mind within my marriage.

I missed the spiritual partnership Jeff and I had once shared and fondly recalled our relationship of many years prior, when both of our hearts had been fully open to one another and exploring the truth within each of us. I walked out of the church feeling empty and lost. I had been holding onto a marriage without a spiritual connection because I still had love for him and didn't want to go through a second divorce and put my kids through the trauma of letting go again. However, I knew then that loving Jeff outside of my heart was never going to work. Until that night, I had been content to wait, thinking that time would change where we had come to in our marriage, returning us to where we had started.

I know now that I was living logically and this was part of the reason I would not allow my finances to flow. I had spiritual partnerships in most areas of my life: with family, friends, and clients. I had worked very hard to release relationships with people who were not mutually willing to share their hearts with me, including clients unwilling to open their hearts. Some clients had only been willing to play the games of the mind, so I had often found myself referring them to other sources or waiting until they were open before engaging in conversation.

Meanwhile, my own husband had been unwilling to do the same, for a long time, yet I had been frightened to let the marriage go for logical reasons. Oddly enough, we got along fine and seemed to have a very normal life, by society's standards, but our hearts were no longer connected, nor did they wish to be, and I finally had to accept this. I needed to let go and embrace my truth with Archangel Michael.

After my experience in the church, my father called me. He asked if I had been thinking about anyone. I laughed and said, "I think of lots of people, why?" Dad knows that many times all I do is think of someone and they call. It's amazing how "God" links people up.

My dad said that a guy named Mike had called for me and had left his number asking that I call him back. It is important to note that Lisa and I have moved many times. Our parents, on the other hand, have had the same telephone number and address since my childhood. I was shocked. Mike was the name of the old boyfriend whose house I had driven past just one-week prior. I wondered if maybe he had heard about the work I was doing and wanted to see if I could help him reconnect with his friend that had passed away so many years earlier.

I called him. To my surprise, he hadn't any idea what I did for a living. In fact, he wasn't sure why he was looking me up after so many years. He said that he simply felt an overwhelming urge to call me. We talked for some time, catching up on the last 19 years, and then, I began telling him of my work with Archangel Michael. He was very interested. In fact, he had had many of the same experiences that I had had. However, he had chosen to shut his connection off many years earlier, due to fear, and had worked very hard at not opening the door because it scared him. Mike is a hearing based person, and like many hearing based intuits that don't understand what they are hearing; he had shut it down, using alcohol and drugs to do so. It can be very disconcerting to hear Spirit if you do not understand that it is indeed Spirit you are hearing.

Mike and I knew that there was a reason we had been reunited after so many years. He was going through a very tough time, questioning what his purpose was in life and without a doubt Archangel Michael had directed our reunion, knowing I could help him answer that question and he could help me feel confidence in my connection to Archangel Michael once again since Jeff and I were essentially divorcing because of it.

Mike is a very gifted intuitive man that doesn't see his gift as a "gift." Archangel Michael also guides Mike; therefore, we share many of the same challenges in our lives, which made it comfortable, from the beginning, for Mike to trust that I could help him. I, however, was not completely sure why he had been brought into my life. Then, one day when I was having a session with him, out of the blue, he said to me, "Did you know that my real name is Anthony?" When he said this, I thought, *Why is he telling me this*?

Two days later, at 6:00 a.m., in a deep sleep, I awoke and sat straight up in bed. Archangel Michael was reminding me of the conversation regarding an old boyfriend named Anthony and of something being incomplete between us. In all these years, I had never known his first name was Anthony. He had always gone by Mike or Michael. It was the confirmation needed from my other friend that my connection is strong.

It all started to sink in. I was beginning to understand what was incomplete between us. As teenagers, Mike had intuitively seen Archangel Michael within me even when I didn't. Nineteen years later he had reached out to renew that connection. Through Mike's unfailing trust, I saw how my connection was indeed a gift instead of a curse. Although, we no longer see each other, I will always be grateful to Mike for helping me find the key to a lifelong commitment to Archangel Michael.

Metaphorically speaking, there are times in our lives when the elevator doors begin to shut and we can put our hand between them to stop them once, twice, or even three times until, finally, when we give up, the doors shut. You are either, then, on the inside, ascending to the next floor, or you will remain on the outside, waiting for the next elevator to arrive. Watching the minister and his fiancée had been my message that it was time to ascend to the next level!

Unfortunately, this was my biggest fear. Letting go of my marriage was an obstacle with which I did not want to deal. Having been brought up in a Catholic environment, I had decided before even my first marriage that divorce was not an acceptable option. However, given Kirk's abuse and adultery, I had been able to justify my first divorce. Now, things were different. I was judging myself enormously and allowing my mind chatter to convince me that if only I continued to follow my heart, everything would work out between Jeff and me; after all, our marriage, on paper, seemed like something that warranted more effort on both of our parts.

My mind was not going to allow me to justify letting go of this marriage as it had in my first. My mind was racing with all the reasons why you hold onto a marriage that looks, by all accounts, wonderful on the outside, yet has no heart.

What I failed to see was that my logical mind had taken over and I was being dogmatic about keeping my marriage together out of beliefs that were not mine. I knew that the love I was experiencing with Jeff was of my mind and that the stability and safety we had had been established through physically being together. Despite all the mind chatter, deep down, I also knew the emptiness in my heart when sitting next to him and sharing space with him. I knew that even when "together," I felt completely isolated and alone; there was no warmth between our hearts.

I knew a change had to be made, so I asked Jeff if he was willing to do anything to transform our situation. His response was, "We see things too differently." I agreed. That was the truth. Our paths had gone in different directions. To stay together, each of us would have had to consciously go against our own truths to make it work, and now I knew that this was something we had been doing unconsciously for years.

I had experienced such a tumultuous divorce the first time around with Kirk that creating and living out a peaceful divorce, while it was our intention, was foreign ground. However, I had taught others what I now had to practice myself: commitment is when you follow the truth of your heart in order to create eternal peace, love, and happiness.

Many people have told me that staying married is the most important thing, even when there is no heartfelt spiritual connection. I disagree. My experience has taught me that you cannot find safety and stability in this world until you look within and allow all of your needs to be met by "God." You will always fall short of any hope of true peace until this has been accomplished.

As said by Jesus, we are to be in the world but not of it, yet we commonly teach our children to do just the opposite. We teach them conceptually that our home, school, and even marriage, all outside sources, is where we find stability and safety. This is why we often find when our so called safety is changed or altered, such as moving to a different home, school or job, and so on, we suffer great anxiety and fear.

This woe does not arise because disruption is wrong, but because we have learned to be reliant upon the world and its stability instead of developing our ability to remain centered with "God" in all circumstances of life. This is a teaching of Michael's that I have to vigilantly keep in my focus. Jacob, Adam, and I have become stronger from our most trying circumstances, having to rely upon our connection to "God" many times, due to "our world" changing so many different times.

It is that false sense of security that lies outside of us which keeps us living in the same houses, neighborhoods, and schools. It creates a cycle that consumes the course of our entire lives. We find ourselves complaining, yet, unable to do anything about it. Some parents will stay in a marriage when the undercurrents of animosity, fear, and even false pleasantries or numbness, to name a few, are so strong that they are destructive to both themselves and their children. They think they are protecting themselves and their children by keeping their outside world consistent, which only maintains an illusion of security.

This is not to say that routine and structure don't have their place. I merely suggest that when you align yourself with "God," you will experience peace, safety, and security in all people and things, no matter what your physical reality dictates.

Eventually, no matter how safe we try to remain when cocooning in our own little worlds, traumatic events will occur that change our perspective: events like divorce, accidents, deaths, and crimes. What I know is that with courage and a lack of judgment, we will all, including our children, find "God" within us during these disruptive times.

My job as a parent is very simple! I acknowledge that I am a human being, making errors nearly every day, but through them, I am learning and growing and all the while, I know that my children's source is within themselves and not in me. I must also direct them at all times back to their heart where Source exists. Had Jacob not gone to his heart where his desire for a dog truly resided, he would not have received Summer. If he instead had looked at his mother, Lynn, as his source, the desire for his dog would not have manifested.

I am concluding this book with a blessing for all humans to consistently follow their heart and live their truth boldly. The "God" inside of you is the greatest gift you can give yourself in this world! Never deny your truth, whether it is through communicating with Archangel Michael, as it is for me, or through being a teacher, singer, actor, business developer, homemaker, or any other truth that lies in your heart, so that you can and will fully experience this world and your human experience.

The final part of this process is not to step beyond judgment; it is to be committed to your truth and to live your life's journey in the *process* of always stepping beyond judgment.

Every day, I am challenged with the judgments of my own logical mind, as well as the logical minds of others in the world that will judge me. Nevertheless, I continue to live without judgment through the love that I receive from "God" and Archangel Michael. My commitment to them gives me the courage to proceed in life, fully expressing myself. Simply put, the final step is being ME.

In the fourth grade, I had to fill out a paper stating my favorite color, food, and various other things about myself, including the answer to the question, "What do you want to be when you grow up?" I ran across this paper recently and was astounded by my answer to that last question. In big bold letters I had written, "ME!" I am pleased to say that I have achieved my heart's desire!

Author's Note:

It has been nearly 20 years since I first wrote this book. So many things have happened and I feel blessed to say that I have continued my work as an Intuitive Educator. My third husband Troy and I have been married now for 16 years, my sons have children of their own and the bliss of being a Nana to these amazing grandchildren is a treasure to behold.

Life, as we all know, is a journey made up of our humanity and spirituality, and thus, it is filled with trials, tribulations, joys, achievements, and so much more. May we all strive to step beyond the judgments of our humanity and embrace the truth of Spirit so integration and unity prevail!

About the Author

Regardless of a person's religious or scientific beliefs, we all have access to a tremendous source of empowerment. Some call these "messages from "God," an "inner voice" or "gut instincts." Lynn has honed her gift to allow Spirit to work through her in assisting others to develop a higher level of consciousness. Once a person has developed a communication to Spirit, the freedom to trust instinctual messages and live a greater experience of life will manifest itself.

As the Founder & CEO of Intuitive Development since 1996, Lynn has shared her natural intuitive abilities to guide people in the awakening of their heart's purpose. Lynn's mission is to provide clear and direct guidance to identify that which is blocking us from living to our fullest potential.

Lynn has consulted with thousands of people from various walks of life and many stages of their own intuitive development. She became a published author with the release of *Stepping Beyond Judgment* and has since developed an extensive on-line curriculum. She celebrated the release of her second book, *Divine Wisdom* in 2008. With a full-time staff and Consultants, Lynn leads The Center for Intuitive Development and currently resides in Phoenix, Arizona with her husband and family.

Made in the USA
Las Vegas, NV
10 May 2022

48688444R00085